Pâtisserie
OF THE EASTERN
MEDITERRANEAN

ARTO DER HAROUTUNIAN

McGRAW-HILL BOOK COMPANY

New York   St. Louis   San Francisco
Hamburg   Mexico

All eggs are large unless otherwise stated

First U.S. publication by McGraw-Hill Book Company in 1989

© Macdonald & Co (Publishers) Ltd 1988

First published in Great Britain in 1988
by Macdonald & Co (Publishers) Ltd
London & Sydney

A member of Maxwell Pergamon Publishing Corporation plc

1 2 3 4 5 6 7 8   8 9 2 1 0 9

Library of Congress Cataloging-in-Publication Data

Der Haroutunian, Arto, *1940–1987.*
Patisserie of the Eastern Mediterranean.
Includes index.
1. Pastry–Middle East.   2. Desserts–Middle East.
I. Title
TX773.D3775   1989   641.865'0956   88-12932

ISBN 0-07-026665-4

Typeset by Tradespools, Frome

Printed and bound in Great Britain by
Purnell Book Production Limited
A member of BPCC plc

Editor: Gillian Prince
Text Editor: Norma MacMillan
Art Director: Bobbie Colegate-Stone
Designer: Frances de Rees
Photographer: Jerry Tubby
Stylist: Sue Russell
Home Economist: Maxine Clark

Contents

Introduction

"Adam was the yeast, Eve the dough." – Armenian saying

It was in Egypt, over four thousand years ago, that "yeast" was first developed. It was used in the fermentation of beer and in the baking of bread. Indeed, it was in Egypt – at that time the most civilized part of the then known world – that our daily eating habits were first formulated, for the Egyptians had breakfast, lunch and supper much as we do in the twentieth century.

In the tomb of Rameses III at Thebes are wall paintings depicting the various activities of an Egyptian kitchen. The cooks are seen kneading dough with their hands, forming it into rolls and then sprinkling the tops with seeds, very much as today. The rich prepared their bread with wheat, while the poor used barley or *doora* (hokus sorghum).

Bread came in varying shapes. The simplest one, a round flat bread, was called *Ta*. Others were triangular or shaped like a heart or a crocodile's head. Sometimes a dough, which was more like a thick batter, was kneaded by feet in a large wooden bowl on the ground, and then formed into thin vermicelli. The process was very much like the modern preparation of Kunafeh Filo (page 121). Two people were engaged in this process. One poured the batter onto a large, hot metal sheet while the other removed it as soon as it was cooked. These filos were then mixed with fruits and other ingredients such as fats, milk, honey and nuts to make pastries. The fruits, of course, were those then available in the area – apples, pomegranates, apricots, olives, and dates. Indeed, we still make a few recipes, such as dates stuffed with pine nuts and cooked in honey, that have ancient roots. In another recipe, Apicius, a first century Mrs. Beeton, advised his readers to cook flour in water till it hardened then, when cold, to cut it into small slices, fry them in oil and pour honey over them before serving. This recipe is the forerunner of all the dry cookies and honey-soaked pastries of the Middle East. Indeed, the vermicelli-type filos depicted at Thebes were probably the progenators of the present-day kunafeh pastries.

The Egyptians, as well as their contemporaries the Mesopotamians and Hittites, soaked dry bread in honey and ate it with milk, much like the fritters and especially the *Ekmek Katayifs* of Anatolia.

Most of the pastries of today did exist in rudimentary forms in ancient times, but over the centuries they have been developed and become more sophisticated. The numerous *halva* dishes, made with flour or semolina which are found throughout North Africa, the

Middle East and as far as India, were known to the people of ancient Akkad as *helou*.

The Arab historian-traveler Ibn Khaldun wrote: "The religion of the king in time becomes that of the people." He could have easily added: "the food of the king in time becomes the food of the people." The truth of this statement is borne out by the fact that the recipes created for the caliphs of Baghdad, as well as the Sultans and Shahs, all in time became the property of the people who also had their own simple cuisine based on the everyday ingredients of their land. Thus, over generations, the various inter-related cuisines of the Middle East were developed so that the Sultans' favorites were equally shared by the desert nomads and the Anatolian farmers.

With the advent of the Arabs, who burst out of the desert dunes of Arabia to conquer in a short time the whole of North Africa and the Middle East, the internationalism of food started. The Arabs incorporated much of the richer cuisines of the newly-conquered races, and the Ottoman Turks, who followed the Arabs, in the same manner cross-fertilized the food and eating habits of their subject races. This is how the *Ghorayebah* pastries of Syrian origin appear throughout the entire region, sometimes with the same name, but often with localized names. Similarly, the Arab *lukmat* (fritters) are found in Greece, the Balkans, Iran and in Turkey where they are in fact at their very best.

Of all the pastries of Middle Eastern origin it is perhaps the Baklavas, and their shredded version Kunafehs, that have come to symbolize the essence of luxury and resplendent living. To quote from *1001 Nights*:

> *Would I not wonder and toil*
> *Seventy years to be able*
> *To eat in Paradise*
> *Kunafeh's subtleties?*

Baklava is first mentioned in the late fifteenth century. Originally it was prepared at Easter. Forty layers of pastry, to represent the 40 days of Lent, were cooked in the oven and then smothered in syrup, to be served on Easter Sunday. Similarly, Kunafeh is first mentioned in the book of recipes of Al-Baghdadi who was most probably of Syrian origin.

Much of the food throughout the Middle East is associated with social and religious festivals. The Christians have 40 days of Lent, as well as Christmas and Easter. The Muslims have their festive days of Ramadan, and the major and minor days of Eid el Kbir; while the Jews have the festivities of the Passover week as well as other important days throughout the year. On all these occasions special pastries are prepared. Similarly, for christenings, weddings and other such social events the village housewives spend long hours baking dishes suitable for that particular occasion.

The ingredients used are those generally readily available. Nuts feature prominently in many sweets. Almonds are very popular in North Africa and Turkey, walnuts in

Armenia and Georgia, pistachios in Syria and Iran, and pine nuts in Lebanon. In certain areas such as the Gulf States cashew nuts are sometimes used.

For sweetness the Ancients used carob juice or honey, and the honey of Greece and Armenia was famous. Today a sugar syrup is the norm, although the North Africans still make much use of honey.

Favorite flavorings are orange blossom water which is especially favored in North Africa, and rosewater which is generally preferred in much of the rest of the Middle East. The spices that give the extra zest to the pastries are cinnamon, nutmeg, cloves, mahleb, mastic and aniseed.

Finally it must be noted that scant use is made of dairy products, barring of course the Turkish and Armenian yoghurt-based pastries. For cream, the Middle Easterners have their own *Kaymak* (page 125). Cream as we know and understand it is little used even today except in such "Western"-style societies as in Israel, Lebanon and the Caucasus.

The pastries of the Middle East will enchant your taste buds, enliven your culinary skills and enrich your appreciation of thousands of years of uninterrupted cultures from ancient Egypt down to our own times.

INGREDIENTS

Tahini: A nutty-flavored paste made from toasted and crushed sesame seeds, tahini is widely available here. The finest quality tahini comes from Syria and Turkey. There are many cheaper versions which tend to be lighter. Tahini separates if it is left to stand, so always stir before using.

Mahleb: This Cilician spice is gathered from the kernel of the black cherry pit. It has a sweet, spicy flavor, is pale brown in color and is the size of a peppercorn. To use, pound it in a mortar and use to flavor breads, cakes and dry cookies. Mahleb can be bought from good Greek and Middle Eastern food stores. There is no real substitute if you cannot obtain it.

Mastic: This is a resin gathered from a small evergreen tree. Most of it comes from the Greek island of Chios. In its powdered form it is used to flavor sweet yeast breads and cakes. As it is both expensive and pungent, I suggest you use it with care. Look for it in Greek and Middle Eastern food stores.

Orange blossom water: A concentrated liquid flavoring distilled from the blossoms of the bitter orange tree. It is used to flavor ice creams, syrups and pastries and is very popular with the Iranians, Turks and North Africans. You can buy it in Middle Eastern and gourmet food stores.

Rosewater: A characteristic fragrance of the Middle Eastern cuisine, rosewater is distilled from rose petals – the finest being the pink-red damask rose. It can be used to flavor puddings, desserts and savories, and can be bought from most Middle Eastern and gourmet food stores. Rosewater essence in a concentrated form known as triple distilled rosewater is also available, but this should be used sparingly in drops rather than spoon measures.

Kunafeh filo: This pastry looks rather like fine shredded wheat or vermicelli. Although I have given a recipe for making it at home (page 121) this is almost impossible to do without a *kunaffahiah*, a special container rather like a sieve with numerous small holes, through which the kunafeh batter is passed onto a hot metal griddle. This pastry is still made in many Middle Eastern households, so anyone visiting these countries may be able to obtain a *kunaffahiah*. For convenience sake it is much easier and quicker to use commercially prepared kunafeh pastry, which is sold in Middle Eastern food stores and some gourmet food stores under the name of kataifi filo. Like baklava filo it should be thawed slowly at room temperature if bought frozen and kept covered with a damp cloth, as it becomes brittle if allowed to dry out. To use, separate the strands carefully with your hands without breaking them and remove any coarse or hard lumps which you may find in some brands.

Nuts: In all cases these should be bought whole from a supplier whose turnover is rapid, as nuts, with their high fat content, quickly become stale and rancid. Pistachio and pine nuts are expensive, but their rich flavor cannot be equalled. Pistachios particularly are often sold salted as a snack, so make sure that you are buying the unsalted variety. Where a recipe calls for ground nuts it is best to grind them yourself in a coffee grinder or nut mill.

Spices: Buy small quantities from stores with a quick turnover – wholefood markets will sell them 1 oz at a time – and use within a few weeks for optimum flavor. Some spices, such as nutmeg, can be bought whole and ground at home.

Tea & Coffee Time Cookies

Filo Pastries

Festive Baklava

ZADGVA BAKLAVA

This version of baklava is the most usual one prepared during Christmas and on Easter Sunday by the Christians of the Middle East. Walnuts are traditionally used in Armenia, Syria and Turkey. However, other nuts such as almonds, pistachios, hazelnuts (filberts) or brazil nuts can be substituted. If you like, add 3–4 tbsp sugar to the filling, and omit the cinnamon.

MAKES ABOUT 24 PIECES

1 cup Clarified Butter (page 123), melted	*Filling*
1 lb package filo pastry or homemade filo (page 120)	½ lb shelled walnuts, chopped or coarsely ground (about 2 cups)
1 quantity Syrup I (page 124)	1 tsp ground cinnamon

Preheat the oven to 350°F. Grease a baking pan, about 12 × 8 × 2 inches, with a little of the melted butter. (You can use other pans of approximately the same area and depth as long as you trim the filo sheets accordingly.)

Carefully open out the stacked sheets of filo pastry and cut in half crosswise. Stack them on top of each other and then cover with wax paper and a damp dish towel to prevent them drying out. Take out two pieces of pastry and re-cover the rest. Lay the two on top of each other in the pan. (Take care not to press on the sheets of filo as they are layered – this will ensure a lighter baklava.) Dribble 1 tbsp of the melted butter over the pastry.

Add two more pieces of filo and dribble another tbsp of butter over. Continue in this way until you have six or eight layers in the pan.

Mix the walnuts and cinnamon together and scatter half of the mixture evenly over the top layer of pastry in the pan.

Add six more layers of filo pastry in the same way, buttering every second one. Sprinkle the remaining nut mixture over the top. Continue to layer and butter the remaining filo in the same way. Brush the top layer of filo thoroughly with butter and pour any that is left over the top.

With a sharp knife, and taking care not to press down on the baklava with your hand, cut into approximately 2 inch square or lozenge shapes. Place in the oven and bake for 30 minutes, then lower the heat to 300°F and bake for a further 1 hour or until golden and cooked through.

Remove from the oven and set aside to cool for 10–15 minutes, then pour the cold syrup evenly over the top. Leave until completely cold, then loosen all the pieces by running a sharp knife along all the gaps.

Baklava with Coconut Filling

BAKLAWA-BIL-JOZ-EL-HIND

MAKES ABOUT 24 PIECES

1 cup Clarified Butter (page 123), melted	*Filling*
	2⅓ cups shredded dried coconut
1 lb package filo pastry or homemade filo (page 120)	6 tbsp sugar
	1 tbsp orange blossom water
3 tbsp finely chopped unsalted pistachio nuts, to garnish	3 tbsp water
	Syrup
	1¾ cups sugar
	1 tbsp lemon juice
	1½ cups water
	3 tbsp orange blossom water
	1 tbsp rosewater

Prepare the syrup by placing the sugar, lemon juice and water in a saucepan and bringing to a boil. Lower the heat and simmer for 10 minutes. Remove from the heat, stir in the orange blossom water and rosewater and set aside to cool.

Preheat the oven to 350°F. Grease a baking pan, about 12 × 8 × 2 inches, with a little of the melted butter. (You can use other pans of approximately the same area and depth as long as you trim the filo sheets accordingly.)

Carefully open out the stacked sheets of filo pastry and cut in half crosswise. Stack them on top of each other and then cover with wax paper and a damp dish towel to prevent them drying out. Take out two pieces of pastry and re-cover the rest. Lay the two on top of each other in the pan. (Take care not to press on the sheets of filo as they are layered.) Dribble 1 tbsp of the melted butter over the pastry.

Add two more pieces of filo and dribble another tbsp of butter over. Continue in this way until you have six or eight layers in the pan.

Mix the filling ingredients together, then sprinkle half evenly over the top layer of pastry in the pan.

Add six more layers of filo pastry in the same way, buttering every second one. Spread the remaining filling over the top. Continue to layer and butter the remaining filo in the same way. Brush the top layer of pastry thoroughly with butter and pour any that remains over the top.

With a sharp knife, and taking care not to press down on the baklava with your hand, cut into approximately 2 inch square or lozenge shapes. Place in the oven and bake for 30 minutes, then lower the heat to 300°F and bake for a further 1 hour or until golden and cooked through.

Remove from the oven and set aside to cool for 10–15 mintues, then pour the cold syrup evenly over the top. Sprinkle with the pistachio nuts. Leave until completely cold, then loosen all the pieces by running a sharp knife along all the gaps.

$\mathcal{F}$ilo Pastry Roll stuffed with Ground Almonds

M'HENCHA

M'hencha – the serpent – is an apt description for this magnificent North African pastry of Berber origin which looks like a large catherine wheel. The pastry is filled with almonds and sugar, rolled and then shaped into a coil. Traditionally ouarka pastry (page 122) is used, but filo pastry is equally suitable although it lacks the thinness of the former. This is a very attractive pastry which is well worth the effort.

SERVES 8

12 sheets filo pastry, bought or homemade (page 120)	*Filling*
	2⅔ cups ground almonds
1 egg yolk	1½ cups confectioners' sugar
Garnish	2 tbsp orange blossom water
3 tbsp confectioners' sugar	4 tbsp unsalted butter, melted
1–2 tsp ground cinnamon	2 large egg yolks, beaten
	2 tsp ground cinnamon

Preheat the oven to 375°F.

Place the ground almonds in a saucepan with the confectioners' sugar, orange blossom water and melted butter and mix to a paste. Cook over a low heat for 10–15 minutes. Remove from the heat. Add one of the egg yolks and the cinnamon and mix thoroughly. Set aside.

Carefully open out the sheets of stacked filo pastry and trim to 12 × 8 inches. Cover with wax paper and a damp dish towel to prevent them drying out.

Take one piece of the filo and lay it out on the work top surface with a long side nearest you. Brush all over with a little of the remaining egg yolk. Lay another piece of pastry on top.

Divide the filling into six equal portions, and place one in a ridge on the pastry, 1½ inches in from the edge nearest you. Take the ridge right out to the two short sides. Fold the 1½ inches of pastry over the filling and then roll up in the rest of the pastry. Brush the top edge with a little egg yolk to stick it down. Repeat with the remaining pastry and filling.

Brush a round baking sheet, about 9–10 inches in diameter, with a little melted butter. Take one roll of pastry and carefully curl it around to form a coil. Place this coil in the middle of the sheet. Take another roll, place one end of it next to the outer end of the coil on the sheet and coil this roll around the first one. Continue using the rolls to extend the coil, sticking the ends of each roll together with a little egg yolk. When all the rolls are on the sheet, brush all over with any remaining egg yolk.

Place in the oven and bake for 25–30 minutes or until golden. Remove from the oven and leave to cool.

Lift onto a serving dish. Sift the confectioners' sugar over the top and decorate with the cinnamon.

Baklava with Sesame Seeds, Pistachios and Raisins

———— BAKLAWAH MIN SEMSEM WAH FISTUK ————

Sesame seeds are much used in the Middle East, particularly in sweets and desserts. An outstanding example is the famed Halva which can be bought in this country. In this recipe the sesame seeds are fried and then mixed with pistachio nuts, raisins and spices to give an unusual earthy flavor. The dessert is a Syrian-Lebanese specialty.

MAKES ABOUT 24 PIECES

1½ cups Clarified Butter (page 123), melted	*Filling*
	⅓ cup sesame seeds
1 lb package filo pastry or homemade filo (page 120)	1½ cups coarsely chopped unsalted pistachio nuts (or almonds or
1 quantity Syrup II (page 124)	hazelnuts (filberts))
	⅓ cup raisins
	6 tbsp sugar
	½ tsp ground cinnamon
	¼ tsp grated nutmeg

Preheat the oven to 350°F. Grease a baking pan, 12 × 8 × 2 inches, with a little of the melted butter.

Place 3 tbsp of the butter in a small pan, add the sesame seeds and fry, stirring frequently, until golden. Remove from the heat, stir in the remaining filling ingredients and set aside.

Carefully open out the stacked sheets of filo pastry and cut in half crosswise. Stack them on top of each other and then cover with wax paper and a damp dish towel to prevent them drying out. Take out two pieces of pastry and re-cover the rest. Lay the two on top of each other in the pan. (Take care not to press on the sheets of filo as they are layered.) Dribble 1 tbsp of melted butter over the pastry.

Add two more pieces of filo and dribble another tbsp of butter over. Continue in this way until you have six or eight layers in the pan. Sprinkle half the filling evenly into the pan.

Add six more layers of filo pastry in the same way, buttering every second one. Sprinkle the remaining filling over the top. Continue to layer and butter the remaining filo in the same way. Brush the top layer of filo thoroughly with butter and pour any that is left over the top.

With a sharp knife, and taking care not to press on the baklava with your hand, cut into approximately 2 inch square or lozenge shapes. Place in the oven and bake for 30 minutes, then lower the heat to 300°F and bake for a further 1 hour or until golden and cooked through.

Remove from the oven and leave to cool for a few minutes, then pour the cold syrup evenly over the top and set aside until completely cold. Loosen all the pieces by running a sharp knife along all the gaps.

Almond and Orange Baklava

———— BADEM VE PORTAKAL BAKLAVASI ————

*I*n Turkey, fruits and nuts are often used as fillings for filo pastry. Eat baklava with fresh fruit-based fillings within a day or two or the pastry will soften.

MAKES ABOUT 24 PIECES

1 cup Clarified Butter (page 123), melted	*Syrup*
	1¾ cups sugar
1 lb package filo pastry or homemade filo (page 120)	1 tbsp lemon juice
	pinch of ground allspice
Filling	1½ cups water
1 lb oranges	3 tbsp orange blossom water
¾ cup coarsely chopped blanched almonds	

First prepare the filling: put the oranges in a large saucepan half-filled with water. Bring to a boil, then lower the heat, cover the pan and leave to simmer for 30 minutes. Drain off the water, add fresh water and bring to a boil. Lower the heat, cover and simmer for a further 30 minutes. Drain and leave to cool.

Quarter the oranges and remove and discard the seeds. Place the quarters in a blender or food processor and process until smooth. Scrape out the pulp and place in a cheesecloth bag. Squeeze out as much liquid as possible. Set the pulp aside to cool.

Prepare the syrup by placing the sugar, lemon juice, allspice and water in a saucepan. Bring to a boil, lower the heat and simmer for 10 minutes. Remove from the heat, stir in the orange blossom water and set aside to cool. Grease a baking pan, about 12 × 8 × 2 inches, with a little of the melted butter.

Carefully open out the stacked sheets of filo pastry and cut in half crosswise. Stack them on top of each other and then cover with wax paper and a damp dish towel to prevent them drying out. Take out two pieces of pastry and re-cover the rest. Lay the two on top of each other in the pan. (Take care not to press on the sheets of filo as they are layered.) Dribble 1 tbsp of melted butter over the pastry.

Continue layering the pastry, buttering every second sheet, until there are 10 layers in the pan.

Mix the orange pulp and chopped almonds together and spread evenly and gently over the filo. Continue to layer and butter the remaining filo until all the pastry has been used. Brush the top layer thoroughly with butter and pour any that is left over the top.

With a sharp knife, and taking care not to press down on the baklava with your hand, cut into approximately 2 inch squares or lozenge shapes. Place in the oven and bake for 30 minutes, then lower the heat to 300°F and bake for a further 1 hour or until golden and cooked through.

Remove from the oven and leave to cool for a few minutes, then pour the cold syrup evenly over the top. Leave until completely cold, then loosen all the pieces by running a sharp knife along all the gaps.

Baklava with Quince and Walnut Filling

—————— SERGEVILOV PAKLAVA ——————

The natural habitat of the quince is the Caucasus and Asia Minor where it has been cultivated for over 3,000 years. It is very popular and widely used in the Middle East. Quinces are rarer here (look for them in the fall), but you can use tart apples instead. Eat within one or two days or the pastry will soften.

MAKES ABOUT 24 PIECES

	Filling
1 cup Clarified Butter (page 123), melted	1 lb peeled quinces, cored
1 lb package filo pastry or homemade filo (page 120)	¾ cup sugar
1 quantity Syrup I (page 124)	1 tsp ground cinnamon
3 tbsp finely chopped unsalted pistachio nuts, to garnish	¾ cup coarsely chopped walnuts

Preheat the oven to 350°F. Grease a baking pan, about 12 × 8 × 2 inches, with a little of the melted butter.

Grate the quinces (there should be about 4 cups) and place in a bowl. Add the sugar and mix well. Put this mixture in a cheesecloth bag or fine dish towel and squeeze out as much juice as possible. Return the grated mixture to the bowl and stir in the cinnamon and walnuts. Set aside.

Carefully open out the stacked sheets of filo pastry and cut in half crosswise. Stack them on top of each other and then cover with wax paper and a damp dish towel to prevent them drying out. Take out two pieces of pastry and re-cover the rest. Lay the two on top of each other in the pan. (Take care not to press on the sheets of filo as they are layered – this will ensure a lighter baklava.) Dribble 1 tbsp of the melted butter over the pastry.

Continue layering the pastry, buttering every second sheet, until there are 10 layers in the pan. Spread the quince filling evenly and gently over the top layer of filo.

Continue to layer and butter the remaining filo in the same way until all the pastry has been used. Brush the top layer thoroughly with melted butter and pour any that is left over the top.

With a sharp knife, and taking care not to press down on the filo with your hand, cut into approximately 2 inch square or lozenge shapes. Place in the oven and bake for 30 minutes, then lower the heat to 300°F and bake for a further 1 hour or until golden and cooked through.

Remove from the oven and leave to cool for a few minutes, then pour the cold syrup evenly over the top. Sprinkle with the pistachio nuts. Leave until completely cold, then loosen all the pieces by running a sharp knife along all the gaps.

Baklava with Pineapple and Pistachio Filling

—— BAHLAWAH-BIL ANANAS WAH FISTUK HALABI ——

Pineapple is not much used in Middle Eastern cooking except in Lebanon and the Gulf States. However, it makes a delicious baklava filling. Eat this within one or two days.

MAKES ABOUT 24 PIECES

1 cup Clarified Butter (page 123), melted	*Filling*
	about 3 cups diced fresh pineapple flesh
1 lb package filo pastry or homemade filo (page 120)	
	⅔ cup finely chopped unsalted pistachio nuts
1 quantity Syrup I (page 124)	

Preheat the oven to 350°F. Grease a baking pan, about 12 × 8 × 2 inches, with a little of the melted butter.

Place the pineapple flesh in a blender or food processor and blend. Transfer the pulp to a cheesecloth bag or fine dish towel and squeeze out as much juice as possible. Reserve the pulp in a bowl.

Carefully open out the stacked sheets of filo pastry and cut in half crosswise. Stack them on top of each other and cover with wax paper and a damp dish towel to prevent them drying out. Take out two pieces of pastry and re-cover the rest. Lay the two on top of each other in the pan. (Take care not to press on the sheets of filo as they are layered – this will ensure a lighter baklava.) Dribble 1 tbsp of the melted butter over the pastry.

Continue layering the pastry, buttering every second sheet, until there are 10 layers in the pan. Stir the chopped pistachio nuts into the pineapple pulp and spread gently and evenly over the top sheet of filo.

Continue to layer the remaining filo, buttering every second sheet, until all the pastry has been used. Brush the top layer thoroughly with butter and pour any that is left over the top.

With a sharp knife, and taking care not to press down on the baklava with your hand, cut into approximately 2 inch square or lozenge shapes. Place in the oven and bake for 30 minutes, then lower the heat to 300°F and bake for a further 1 hour or until golden and cooked through.

Remove from the oven and leave to cool for a few minutes, then pour the cold syrup evenly over the top. Leave until completely cold, then loosen all the pieces by running a sharp knife along all the gaps.

$\mathscr{L}$ayers of Filo Pastry with Almonds and Custard Cream

BASTELA

SERVES 6–8

24 sheets North African Paper-Thin Pastry (page 122) or filo pastry, bought or homemade (page 120)	*Cream mixture*
	3 eggs, separated
	5 cups milk
oil for frying	1 tbsp vanilla extract
2 tbsp clear honey, to finish	¾ cup sugar
	1 tbsp all-purpose flour
	Almond mixture
	3 tbsp vegetable oil
	1½ cups finely chopped blanched almonds
	½ cup sugar

To prepare the cream mixture, put the egg whites in a bowl and beat until stiff. Place the milk and vanilla in a saucepan, bring to a boil and remove from the heat. Drop spoonfuls of the egg white into the milk. Poach for 2 minutes. Remove with a slotted spoon and reserve. Poach the remaining egg white.

In another bowl, beat the egg yolks and sugar together until white. Gradually beat in the flour and continue to beat for 2–3 minutes. Slowly stir in a little of the hot milk until runny, then stir this mixture into the milk pan. Return to the heat and simmer for 3–4 minutes, stirring constantly. Remove from the heat and cool. The cream should be of a pouring consistency. Add a little milk if necessary.

For the almond mixture, heat the oil in a small pan, add the chopped almonds and fry until golden. Remove with a slotted spoon, drain and place in a small bowl. Stir in the sugar and set aside.

Place a 9 inch diameter plate on top of the stacked pastry sheets and trim around it to make rounds. Cover with wax paper and a damp dish towel to prevent the pastry drying out.

Heat some oil in a large skillet and, one by one, fry the pastry rounds until golden, turning once. Remove with a slotted spoon and drain on paper towels. When they are all cooked, pile on top of each other and keep warm in a low oven until ready to serve.

To assemble the Bastela, place two pastry rounds on top of each other in a large shallow serving dish. Sprinkle with a little of the almond mixture, then add another round of pastry. Spoon a little of the cream mixture over it. Add another pastry round and sprinkle with almonds. Continue these layers until all the pastry and almonds have been used. When the last piece of pastry has been stacked, pour any remaining cream over the top, arrange the poached egg whites over it and dribble with the honey. Serve immediately.

Illustrated on page 22

Filo Pastries filled with Custard Cream

──────── GALATABOURIKO ────────

MAKES 16

8 sheets filo pastry, bought or homemade (page 120)	*Syrup*
	¾ cup sugar
3 tbsp unsalted butter, melted	1 tbsp lemon juice
Filling	2 cups water
3¾ cups milk	3 tbsp orange blossom water
1¼ cups sugar	
1 cup rice flour	
2 sticks (8 oz) unsalted butter, cut into small pieces	
1 heaped tbsp finely grated orange zest	
6 eggs, separated	
pinch of salt	

Preheat the oven to 350°F.

First prepare the filling: pour the milk into a saucepan and add ¾ cup of the sugar and the rice flour. Add the pieces of butter and cook over a moderate heat, stirring constantly, until the mixture has a custard-like consistency. Stir in the orange zest and pour into a large bowl. Set aside to cool.

Beat the egg whites with the salt until stiff. Place the egg yolks in another bowl with the remaining sugar and beat until pale and creamy. Fold the whites and yolks quickly but gently into the custard.

Carefully open out the stacked sheets of filo pastry and cut in half crosswise. Stack them on top of each other and cover with wax paper and a damp dish towel to prevent them drying out.

Take one piece of the pastry and lay it flat on the work surface. Place 2 tbsp of the custard filling in a ridge about 5 inches long and 2½ inches in from the edge nearest you. Fold the edge of the pastry over the filling, fold the two sides in over the ends of the filling and roll the pastry up carefully and loosely (filling will expand while cooking). Repeat until you have used up all the ingredients.

Grease two large baking sheets with a little of the melted butter and arrange the pastries, seams underneath, at least 1 inch apart, on them. Brush the pastries with melted butter.

Place in the center of the oven and bake for 30–40 minutes or until puffed up and light golden. Cool.

To prepare the syrup, place the sugar, lemon juice and water in a saucepan and bring to a boil. Simmer for 10 minutes, then remove from the heat and stir in the orange blossom water.

Pour the syrup evenly over the galatabouriko and leave until cold.

Illustrated on page 23

Layers of Filo Pastry with Almonds and Custard Cream

Filo Pastries filled with Custard Cream

$\mathcal{F}$ilo Pastry and Apple Twists, Palace-Style

—————— SARAY ELMALI BURMA ——————

"An apple gets its color from seeing another apple." – Afghan saying

hese, and many similar pastries, were developed over the centuries in the Ottoman Court for the gratification of the Sultans and their entourages. Traditionally the filo pastry used for this and similar pastries is thicker then baklava filo, so I suggest you use a double thickness of baklava filo. This recipe is for apple twists, but other fruits such as cherries, quinces and oranges can be used as well as nuts.

MAKES 30–36

		Filling	
½ lb filo pastry, bought or homemade (page 120)		½ lb apples, peeled, cored and grated	
½ cup Clarified Butter (page 123), melted		½ cup sugar	
		½ cup raisins	
		½ tsp ground cinnamon	
		Syrup	
		2¼ cups sugar	
		2½ cups water	
		juice of 1 lemon	

Preheat the oven to 350°F.

First prepare the syrup by putting the sugar, water and lemon juice in a saucepan and bringing to a boil. Lower the heat and simmer for 10 minutes. Set aside to cool.

Place the grated apple in a cheesecloth bag or fine dish towel and squeeze out as much juice as possible. Transfer the pulp to a bowl and stir in the sugar, raisins and cinnamon.

Carefully open out the stacked filo and cover with wax paper and a damp dish towel to prevent it drying out. Take one sheet, lay it on the work surface and brush its surface with melted butter. Lay another sheet of pastry on top. Place a long thin rolling pin or stick about ½ inch in diameter 1 inch in from one of the shorter ends. Sprinkle a little of the filling evenly all along the inner edge of the stick. Carefully fold the outside edge of the pastry over the stick and then roll the stick over the filling. Fold over once more and then brush the edge with butter. Fold over once more and cut along the edge with a knife. Do not fold more than four times. You should get three rolls from each doubled sheet of pastry.

Carefully push in both ends of the rolled pastry toward the center to make the roll smaller and to create wrinkles and folds. Take care or the filling will burst through the pastry. Gently pull out the stick. Transfer the roll to a buttered baking sheet, with the seam underneath. Continue in this way until you have used up all the pastry and filling.

Brush the tops of the pastries with any remaining butter. Place in the oven and bake for about 30 minutes or until golden. Remove from the oven and set aside to cool for 10–15 minutes.

Cut each pastry in half and pour the syrup over them. Set aside to cool completely before serving.

"*Bird's Nest" Filo Pastries in Syrup*

———————— SUARZES ————————

These are light, cigarette-thin pastries covered in syrup. They are a specialty from Northern Syria which is also popular in Southern Turkey where they are called Antep Suarzesi. In appearance, Suarzes look like miniature bird's nests with the golden pastry contrasting with the green of the chopped pistachios.

MAKES 42

7 sheets filo pastry, bought or homemade (page 120)
¾ cup Clarified Butter (page 123), melted
1 quantity hot Syrup I (page 124)
¼ cup very finely chopped unsalted pistachio nuts, to garnish

Preheat the oven to 325°F.

Lay the sheets of pastry out flat, one on top of the other. Mark the top one down through the middle lengthwise and divide crosswise into three equal parts, thus dividing it into six portions. Cut down along these markings through all seven sheets, then stack all 42 pieces of pastry on top of each other and cover with wax paper and a damp dish towel to prevent them drying out.

Take one piece of pastry, lay it flat and brush its surface all over with melted butter. Roll it up as you would a cigarette. Carefully bend the roll into a circle and squeeze the two ends together. They will stick easily if you dampen your fingers first. Repeat with all the remaining pieces of pastry.

Lightly grease large baking sheets and arrange the Suarzes about ½ inch apart on them. Brush the pastries with the remaining melted butter, then place in the oven and bake for 20–25 minutes or until light golden in color.

Pour the hot syrup over the Suarzes as they come out of the oven, then leave until cold.

Arrange the pastries on a large serving dish, sprinkle with the chopped nuts and serve.

Illustrated on page 27

Filo Pastry Rolls with Cheese and Raisins

——— KOROGLU PEYNIR SARMASI ———

I suggest you try feta, ricotta or a similar crumbly white cheese for these pastries. If using feta cheese, soak it first for 12 hours in cold water, changing the water several times, to remove excess salt and then drain.

MAKES 30–36

1 lb package filo pastry or homemade filo (page 120)	*Syrup*
	2½ cups water
1 cup Clarified Butter (page 123), melted	2¼ cups sugar
	juice of 1 lemon
Filling	*Garnish*
1 lb white cheese	2 tbsp finely chopped unsalted
½ cup raisins	pistachio nuts
scant ½ cup finely chopped dried dates	2 tbsp shredded dried coconut

Preheat the oven to 350°F. Cut the cheese into ¼ inch cubes, place in a bowl and stir in the raisins and dates.

Carefully open out the stacked filo and cover with wax paper and a damp dish towel to prevent it drying out. Take out one sheet, lay it flat and brush with some melted butter. Lay another sheet on top.

Take a long thin rolling pin about ½ inch thick (or even a thick knitting needle or piece of cane) and lay it 1 inch from one of the shorter sides. Sprinkle a little of the filling evenly along the inner edge of the pin. Carefully fold the edge of the pastry over the pin and filling and then roll the pin over the filling. Fold over once more and then brush a narrow strip of pastry along the edge of the rolling pin with butter. Fold over once more and then cut along the edge with a knife.

Carefully push in both ends of the rolled pastry toward the middle to create wrinkles and folds. Gently pull out the rolling pin, then place the pastry, with its seam underneath, on a buttered baking sheet.

Continue to prepare the pastries until all the ingredients are used up. You should be able to make three pastries from each doubled sheet of filo.

Arrange the pastries closely together on baking sheets and brush the tops with any remaining butter. Bake for about 30 minutes or until golden.

Meanwhile, prepare the syrup by placing the water, sugar and lemon juice in a saucepan and bringing to a boil. Simmer for 10–15 minutes and then set aside.

When the pastries are cooked, remove them from the oven and leave to cool for 10 minutes. Cut each pastry in half and pour the warm syrup over them. Sprinkle with the pistachio nuts and the coconut. Set aside to cool completely before serving.

"Bird's Nest" Filo Pastries in Syrup (left)   27
Filo Pastry Rolls with Cheese and Raisins (right)

Shredded Filo Pastries

Poor Man's Shredded Pastry in Syrup

KUNAFAT EL FUKHARI

The caliph's poets may have sung the praises of "Kunaph's sweetness" filled with nuts, spices or fruits, but the poor folk had to be content with the pastry alone soaked in syrup. This is the simplest kunafeh of all yet it is still marvelous to taste. Try it and see!

MAKES ABOUT 24 PIECES

1 lb kunafeh pastry, bought or homemade (page 121)	*Garnish*
1½ cups Clarified Butter (page 123), melted	3 tbsp finely chopped unsalted pistachio nuts or shredded dried coconut
1 quantity Syrup I (page 124)	1 tsp ground cinnamon

Preheat the oven to 350°F.

Put the pastry in a large bowl and gently ease apart the strands without breaking them. Remove any hard nodules of pastry, which you may find in some brands. Pour three-quarters of the melted butter into the bowl and gently rub the strands of pastry between your palms until they are all coated with butter.

Divide the pastry into four equal parts. Taking one at a time, spread them out on the work surface and gently roll up with your hands. The rolls should be about 1½ inches in diameter. With a sharp knife cut each roll across into approximately 4 inch lengths.

Brush a baking pan, about 12 × 9 inches, with a little of the melted butter and arrange the rolls in the pan. Brush the tops with any remaining butter. Place in the oven and bake for about 40 minutes or until golden.

Remove and pour the cold syrup evenly over the rolls. Set aside to cool and then sprinkle with the pistachios or coconut and the cinnamon.

Serve cold with fresh cream.

Shredded Pastry, Festive-Style

KUNAFAT EL EID

Prepared during the Muslim festival of Eid, as well as during the Christian Christmas and New Year week, this pastry is excellent on its own or with cream. Traditionally the filling was chopped walnuts, but hazelnuts (filberts), almonds, pistachios and so on are equally suitable.

MAKES 24–30 PIECES

1 lb kunafeh pastry, bought or homemade (page 121)	*Filling*
	6 oz shelled walnuts, chopped or coarsely ground (about 1½ cups)
1½ cups Clarified Butter (page 123), melted	
	2 tbsp sugar
1 quantity Syrup I (page 124)	2 tsp ground cinnamon

Preheat the oven to 350°F. Grease a baking pan, about 12 × 8 inches or about 10 inches in diameter and at least 1 inch deep, with a little of the melted butter.

Put the pastry in a large bowl and gently ease apart the strands without breaking them. Remove any hard nodules of pastry, which you may find in some brands. Pour three-quarters of the melted butter into the bowl and gently rub the strands of pastry between your palms until they are all coated with butter.

Divide the pastry into two equal parts and spread one of them evenly over the bottom of the pan.

Mix the filling ingredients together in a small bowl and sprinkle evenly into the pan. Press down firmly. Arrange the remaining pastry over the filling and tuck in any loose strands along the edges. Press down firmly with your hands. Spoon any remaining butter evenly over the top.

Place in the oven and bake for 30 minutes, then lower the heat to 300°F and bake for a further 1–1½ hours or until cooked and golden.

Remove from the oven and pour the cold syrup evenly over the surface. Cover with foil, place a board over the top and add a heavy weight in order to compact the sweet. Leave until cold and then cut into 1½–2 inch square or lozenge shapes.

$\mathcal{S}$hredded Pastry with Nuts, Rosewater and Orange Blossom Water

KUNAFEH MAFROUKE

This pastry is shredded into tiny portions, flavored with rosewater and orange blossom water, topped with fried nuts and lavishly garnished with spiced confectioners' sugar. It is easy to prepare, good to look at and delicious. Eat on the day it is prepared.

SERVES 6–8

½ cup Clarified Butter (page 123), melted
¼ cup shelled unsalted pistachio nuts
scant ¼ cup blanched almonds
⅓ cup pine nuts
½ lb kunafeh pastry, bought or homemade (page 121)
1 tbsp rosewater
1 tbsp orange blossom water
1 cup confectioners' sugar
1 tsp ground cinnamon

Melt half the butter in a small pan, add the pistachio nuts and fry, stirring frequently, until golden. Remove with a slotted spoon, drain on paper towels and reserve. Fry the almonds and then the pine nuts in the same way.

Place the shredded pastry in a large bowl and tear apart the strands until they are about the size of rice grains. Alternatively, pass the pastry through a meat grinder.

Melt the remaining butter in a large saucepan. Add the pastry and, over a low heat, rub the butter into the pastry until all the strands are as fine as possible and coated with butter. Remove from the heat and set aside to cool.

Add the rosewater and orange blossom water to the pastry and mix thoroughly. Sift the confectioners' sugar and cinnamon together and stir three-quarters of it into the pastry.

Pile the pastry into a serving dish and sprinkle the fried nuts over it. Dust with the remaining spiced sugar and serve with cream.

Shredded Pastry filled with Cherries and Coconut

KIRAZLI TEL-KATAYIF

"The man who is not hungry says coconut has a hard shell." – Egyptian saying

For this recipe you should use fresh cherries, but large canned Morello-type cherries will do instead. There is a marvelous combination of colors here – the gold of the pastry, pink of the coconut and deep red of the cherry pulp. The taste is also delicious.

MAKES 24–30 PIECES

1 lb kunafeh pastry, bought or homemade (page 121)	*Filling*
	½ lb (about 1 pint), cherries, pitted
1 cup Clarified Butter (page 123), melted	scant 1 cup shredded dried coconut
	1 tsp vanilla extract
1 quantity Syrup II (page 124)	

Preheat the oven to 350°F. Lightly brush a baking pan, about 12 × 8 inches and at least 1 inch deep, with a little of the melted butter.

To prepare the filling, either chop the cherries finely or pass them through a meat grinder. Place in a bowl and stir in the coconut and vanilla. Set aside.

Put the pastry in a large bowl. Remove any hard nodules that may occur with some brands. Pull the strands apart gently, then pour in three-quarters of the melted butter. Rub between your palms until all the pastry is well coated.

Spread half the pastry over the bottom of the pan, then spread the filling evenly over it. Arrange the remaining pastry over the filling and tuck in any loose strands. Press the pastry down firmly and pour the rest of the butter evenly over the top.

Place in the oven and bake for 30 minutes, then lower the heat to 300°F and bake for a further 1–1½ hours or until golden and cooked.

Remove from the oven and pour the cold syrup evenly over the surface of the sweet. Cover with foil, place a board and heavy weight on top and set aside until cold. Cut into 1½–2 inch squares for serving.

Illustrated on page 34

White Kunafeh

———— BALOURIEH ————

This is understandably the queen of all Kunafehs. It is a specialty of Aleppo in Northern Syria. The pastry is cooked in such a way as to remain white. This contrasts brilliantly with the green of the pistachio nuts.

MAKES 24–30 PIECES

⅔ cup Clarified Butter (page 123), melted	*Filling*
1 tbsp clear honey	6 oz shelled unsalted pistachio nuts, coarsely chopped (1 cup)
1 lb kunafeh pastry, bought or homemade (page 121)	3 tbsp sugar
	1 tsp ground cinnamon
2 tbsp very finely chopped unsalted pistachio nuts, to garnish	*Syrup*
	2¼ cups sugar
	2 cups water
	1 tbsp lemon juice

Preheat the oven to 300°F.

Pour the melted butter into a bowl and refrigerate until semi-solid. Remove, add the honey and beat until frothy. Pour into a baking pan, about 12 × 8 inches and at least 1 inch deep. Swirl around to coat the bottom and sides.

Spread out the pastry on the work surface. Divide it into four portions and, taking one at a time, squeeze between the palms of your hands for 2–3 minutes to loosen the strands. Take two of the portions and gently ease the strands out without breaking them. Spread evenly over the bottom of the pan.

Mix the filling ingredients together in a bowl and spread evenly over the pastry in the pan. Gently ease apart the remaining two portions of pastry and arrange them over the filling. Press the pastry down firmly and tuck in any loose strands.

Place in the oven and bake for 20 minutes, keeping the door ajar – this will prevent the pastry from changing color. Remove from the oven. Lift the pan at an angle and carefully pour off the butter and honey mixture into a bowl. Completely cover the sweet with a large tray or board and turn it over. Carefully slide the sweet back into the pan, return to the oven and, still with the door ajar, bake for a further 20 minutes.

Meanwhile, make the syrup by placing the sugar, water and lemon juice in a saucepan. Bring to a boil and boil vigorously for 5 minutes, then remove from the heat.

Remove the sweet from the oven. Bring the syrup back to a boil and pour evenly over the surface of the sweet. To give the sweet its compact appearance, cover it with foil, place a board or tray over it and press down with a heavy weight until the Balourieh is cold.

Cut into 1½–2 inch squares and sprinkle with the finely chopped pistachios before serving.

Illustrated on page 35

Shredded Pastry filled with Cherries and Coconut

White Kunafeh

Rolled Shredded Pastry filled with Pistachio Nuts

—— BURMA TEL-KATAYIF ——

Mabrouma in Arabic means "to twist" or "whirl" – hence the Turkish word burma. This is a rich dry pastry packed full of pistachios, the green color of which contrasts sharply with the dark gold of the pastry.

MAKES 15–18 PIECES

1 lb kunafeh pastry, bought or homemade (page 121)	*Filling*
	¾ lb shelled unsalted pistachio nuts
1½ cups Clarified Butter (page 123), melted	¾ cup finely chopped blanched almonds
1 quantity Syrup I (page 124)	3 tbsp sugar

Preheat the oven to 350°F.

Put the pastry in a large bowl and gently pull the strands apart without tearing them. Remove any hard nodules of pastry, which you may find in some brands. Divide into three equal portions. Take one of the portions and gently pull it out and flatten it as much as possible with your hands, until about ¼–½ inch thick and 12 × 6 inches. Brush the surface very generously with some of the melted butter. Take a flat stick about 18 inches long and 1 inch wide and lay it diagonally across the flattened pastry.

Mix the filling ingredients together in a small bowl and spread one-third of it evenly along the stick. Roll the pastry up around the stick as tightly as possible. Hold the roll tightly in one hand and gently pull the stick out, leaving the filling inside. Brush some more melted butter all over the roll and place on a lightly buttered baking sheet. Repeat with the remaining pastry and filling.

Pour the remaining butter evenly over the rolls. Place in the oven and bake for 30 minutes, then lower the heat to 300°F and bake for a further 1–1½ hours or until cooked and golden.

Remove from the oven and pour the cold syrup evenly over the rolls, turning each one several times so that it is well covered. Set aside until cold and then cut diagonally into 2–3 inch pieces.

$\mathcal{S}$hredded Pastry with Cheese Filling

───────── PEYNIRLI TEL KATAYIF ─────────

*T*he filling for this pastry is best prepared with a goat's cheese called bolu. However, since this is
virtually unobtainable outside Turkey (indeed it is even rather difficult to find it there!) I suggest
one of the following instead: akkawe, ricotta or any other sweet white cheese. If you want to use feta,
soak it in cold water for several hours first – this helps to remove the excess salt.

MAKES ABOUT 24 PIECES

⅔ cup Clarified Butter (page 123), melted	*Filling*
	¾ lb sweet white cheese
1 lb kunafeh pastry, bought or homemade (page 121)	1 tbsp rosewater
1 quantity Syrup II (page 124), made with 2¼ cups sugar and 2 cups water	

Preheat the oven to 325°F. Lightly grease a baking pan, about 12 × 8 inches and at least 1 inch deep, with some of the butter.

Grate the cheese, place in a bowl and stir in the rosewater.

Put the pastry in a large bowl and gently pull apart the strands, breaking them into smaller pieces. Remove any hard nodules, which you may find in some brands. Pour the remaining butter over the pastry and rub the strands between your palms until they are all coated with the butter.

Spread half the pastry evenly over the bottom of the pan, then spread the cheese mixture over it. Arrange the remaining pastry evenly over the filling and tuck in any loose strands. Press the pastry down lightly.

Place in the oven and bake for about 45 minutes or until light golden. Remove from the oven, place a larger pan over the top and invert, to turn the sweet over into the larger pan. Return to the oven and bake for a further 30–45 minutes or until golden.

Remove from the oven and either pour over the syrup immediately or leave to cool and serve with the syrup in a separate container. Cut into 2 inch squares for serving.

$\mathcal{S}$*hredded Pastry Mounds*

KIZ MEMESI TEL-KATAYIF

$\mathcal{S}$mall, firm, rounded pastries topped with half a walnut, these are called "young girl's breasts" by the Turks – a nation which, more than any other in the Middle East, brought sensuality into food. It was, of course, the Sultans and viziers for whom such delicious pastries were first created.

MAKES ABOUT 12

1 lb kunafeh pastry, bought or homemade (page 121)	*Syrup*
	2¼ cups sugar
1 cup Clarified Butter (page 123), melted	2 cups water
	1 tbsp lemon juice
about 12 walnut halves	
¾ cup finely chopped blanched almonds	

Preheat the oven to 350°F.

Place the pastry in a large bowl and pull apart the strands, discarding any coarse lumps you may find in some brands. Shred the pastry very finely with your fingers or pass through a meat grinder. Pour in most of the melted butter and rub the pastry between your palms until it is all coated with butter.

Lightly brush two baking sheets with a little of the remaining butter.

To make this pastry the correct shape you need a soup ladle or container of similar shape and size, about 2½ inches in diameter. Brush the inside of the ladle with melted butter and put a walnut half in the bottom. Fill the ladle with shredded pastry and make a hole with your index finger into the center of the pastry. Fill the hole with 1–2 tsp of the chopped nuts and then add a little more pastry to cover the nuts. Press down firmly. Place your fingers over the mouth of the ladle, turn it over and slide the pastry out. Place on the baking sheet. Continue until you have used up all the ingredients.

Place in the oven and bake for 40 minutes.

Meanwhile prepare the syrup by placing the sugar, water and lemon juice in a saucepan and bring to a boil. Simmer for 10 minutes, then set aside.

When the pastries are cooked, remove them from the oven. Bring the syrup back to a boil and ladle it over the pastries. Set aside to cool before serving.

Doughnuts & Fritters

Armenian "Ear-Shaped" Pastry Fritters

AGANCHK

These simple pastry twists are delicately flavored, fried in oil and then dusted with confectioners' sugar and finely chopped pistachio nuts. Both the Caucasian and Iranian cuisines are rich with such pastries as these.

MAKES 30–34

1 egg	*Garnish*
2 tbsp butter, melted	confectioners' sugar
½ cup sugar	2 tbsp finely chopped unsalted
2 tbsp brandy	pistachio nuts
1⅔ cups all-purpose flour	
oil for deep-frying	

Place the egg, butter and sugar in a large bowl and beat together until well blended. Stir in the brandy. Sift in the flour and stir until the mixture holds together. Transfer to a lightly floured work surface and knead until smooth.

Flour the work surface again and roll out the dough as thinly as possible. Use a 4 inch cutter to cut out as many rounds of dough as possible. Cut each round in half. Taking one at a time, pleat the straight edge and then press together to form an "ear" shape. Repeat with the remaining half moons of dough.

Cover the "ears" with a clean cloth and leave to rest for 30 minutes.

Heat enough oil to deep-fry in a large pan to 350°F. Drop three or four pastries into the oil and fry gently for 2–3 minutes, turning once, until golden. Remove with a slotted spoon and drain on paper towels. Keep warm while you fry the remaining pastries in the same way.

Arrange the "ears" on a serving plate and dust generously with confectioners' sugar. Garnish with the chopped pistachio nuts and serve warm or cold.

Illustrated on page 42

"*Lady's Navel*" *Fritters*

——— HAMIN GOBEGI ———

*T*hese delicious doughnuts make an impressive dessert. They are dipped in syrup and topped with whipped cream. The depression in the middle of each is meant to represent a lady's navel – thus their unusual name!

MAKES 12–16

4 tbsp butter	*Syrup*
1¼ cups water	2¼ cups sugar
1⅔ cups all-purpose flour, sifted	1 tbsp lemon juice
½ tsp salt	2 cups water
3 eggs	
oil for deep-frying	
about 1 tsp almond extract	
¾ cup heavy cream, whipped, to finish	

First prepare the syrup: place the sugar, lemon juice and water in a saucepan and bring to a boil. Lower the heat and simmer for 10 minutes, then set aside to cool.

Place the butter in a saucepan with the water and bring to a boil, stirring all the time until the butter melts. Remove from the heat, add the flour and salt and, using a wooden spoon, stir vigorously until the mixture is well blended. Make a well in the center of the dough and add the eggs, one at a time, beating until the mixture is smooth and shiny and comes away from the sides of the pan.

Lightly oil your hands. Break off walnut-sized lumps of dough, roll between your palms to form balls and place well apart on an oiled baking sheet.

Heat sufficient oil in a large saucepan to deep-fry to 350°F.

Flatten two or three balls a little, dip your forefinger into the almond extract and press it about ½ inch into the center of each ball to make a depression. Place the doughnuts into the gently sizzling oil and leave to fry for about 8 minutes. Turn once and fry for a further 8 minutes or until evenly golden. Do not fry too quickly or the doughnuts will not be cooked through. Remove with a slotted spoon and drain on paper towels. Drop into the syrup, turn once and leave for 5 minutes before removing with a slotted spoon to a serving plate.

Continue until all the doughnuts are fried and steeped in syrup.

Before serving place a little cream into the depression in each doughnut.

Illustrated on page 43

Armenian "Ear-Shaped" Pastry Fritters

"Lady's Navel" Fritters

 Raisin Doughnuts

──── SFENAJ ────

These tasty doughnuts are found in Morocco and Algeria. They are often eaten for breakfast, but are delicious at any other time as well!

MAKES 16

½ oz compressed yeast, or 1 package active dry yeast

1 tsp sugar

1¼ cups lukewarm water

3¼ cups all-purpose flour

pinch of salt

⅓ cup raisins

oil for deep-frying

confectioners' sugar or Syrup I or II (page 124), to finish

Place the yeast and sugar in a small bowl with a little of the warm water. If compressed yeast, cream together; if dry, stir to dissolve. Leave in a warm place for 15–20 minutes or until the mixture begins to froth.

Sift the flour and salt into a large bowl and stir in the raisins. Make a well in the center and pour in the yeast mixture. Gradually work in enough of the remaining water to make a soft dough. Gather into a ball and knead on a lightly floured work surface for at least 10 minutes or until soft and elastic. (Alternatively, knead the dough using the dough hook in a heavy duty (countertop) electric mixer.) Place in a clean bowl, cover with a dish towel and leave in a warm place to rise for about 2 hours or until doubled in bulk.

Heat enough oil in a large pan to deep-fry to 350°F.

Lightly flour your hands and divide the dough into 16 lumps. Taking one lump at a time, roll it into a ball, flatten it a little and make a hole through the center with your index finger. Cook the doughnuts a few at a time in the oil over a medium heat for 8–10 minutes or until golden, turning once. Do not fry too quickly or the insides will not be thoroughly cooked. Remove with a slotted spoon and drain on paper towels.

Serve warm or cold, dredged with sifted confectioners' sugar or dipped into a syrup.

Tunisian Orange Doughnuts

YO-YO

A delicious Tunisian version of the doughnut, this exudes a wonderful aroma due to the clever combination of orange and honey – two ingredients found in abundance in North Africa.

MAKES ABOUT 12

2 eggs	*Syrup*
3 tbsp oil	1 cup + 2 tbsp sugar
3 tbsp fresh orange juice	1 tbsp lemon juice
1 tbsp finely grated orange zest	1¼ cups water
¼ cup sugar	⅓ cup honey
1⅔ cups all-purpose flour	
2 tsp baking soda	
oil for deep-frying	

Place the eggs, oil, and orange juice and zest in a large bowl with the sugar and whisk until well blended. Gradually sift in the flour and soda and beat until the mixture is smooth. Set the dough aside while you prepare the syrup.

Place the sugar, lemon juice and water in a pan and bring to a boil. Lower the heat and simmer for 5–7 minutes. Add the honey and stir until it dissolves, then simmer for a further 5 minutes. Remove from the heat and set aside.

Heat sufficient oil in a large pan to deep-fry to 350°F.

Lightly flour your palms and shape the dough into 2 inch balls. Taking one at a time, press between your palms to flatten slightly and make a hole through the center with your index finger. Drop two or three doughnuts at a time into the oil and cook gently for 7–10 minutes, turning once, until golden and cooked through. Remove with a slotted spoon and drain on paper towels. Drop into the warm syrup and leave to soak up as much syrup as possible.

Arrange on a large plate and keep warm while you prepare the remaining doughnuts in the same way.

Greek Deep-Fried Sweet Pastries

THIPLES

A *Greek version of a pastry found throughout the Middle East. There are various ways of folding the pastry, but the most attractive one produces pastries shaped rather like roses.*

MAKES 24–30

3 eggs	*Topping*
2 tbsp sugar	⅔ cup clear honey, warmed
1 tsp baking powder	¼ lb shelled walnuts or blanched
pinch of salt	almonds, finely chopped (about 1
juice of ½ lemon	cup), or ¾ cup toasted sesame seeds
1⅔ cups all-purpose flour	ground cinnamon
oil for deep-frying	

Place the eggs in a large bowl and beat until frothy. Add the sugar, baking powder and salt and beat until the mixture thickens. Stir in the lemon juice.

Sift the flour into the bowl and stir until a dough is formed. Transfer to a well floured work surface and knead for a few minutes. The dough should be a little sticky. Divide the dough into two balls, roll in a little flour, wrap in foil and refrigerate for 1–2 hours.

Taking one ball at a time, unwrap, place on a floured work surface and roll out as thinly as possible, taking care not to let the pastry stick to the work surface. Cut into strips about ¾ inch wide and 20 inches long. Taking one strip at a time, pinch the long edges together at ¾ inch intervals. Keeping flat, fold in half, then coil loosely, pinching the edges together firmly at intervals to prevent it unwinding during cooking.

Alternatively you can cut the pastry into 2 inch squares and fold into triangles. Keep the shapes covered with a dish towel while you prepare all the pastry in the same way.

Heat enough oil to deep-fry in a large pan to 350°F. When ready, add two or three pastries at a time and fry for about 1 minute, turning once, until evenly golden. Remove with a slotted spoon and drain on paper towels while the remaining pastries are cooked in the same way.

Arrange a layer of pastries on a serving plate, dribble honey into the center of each and sprinkle with the nuts or sesame seeds and cinnamon. Arrange more layers on top, garnishing each in the same way. Spoon any extra honey over the top.

Pastries

Israeli Tahini Pastries with Nut Filling

TAHINA IM EGOZIM

*N*ot to be outdone, the Israeli cuisine, of much more recent vintage, has developed these tasty, nut-filled tahini balls. They are delicious with tea or coffee.

MAKES ABOUT 20

2⅓ cups all-purpose flour	*Filling*
pinch of salt	¼ lb shelled walnuts, ground
1 stick butter or margarine	(about 1⅓ cups)
¼ cup sugar	2 tbsp finely chopped dates
	½ tsp ground cinnamon
	1½ tbsp sugar
	3 tbsp tahini (page 8)
	Topping
	1 egg, beaten
	sesame seeds

Preheat the oven to 350°F.

Prepare the filling by mixing all the ingredients together in a bowl.

Sift the flour and salt into a large bowl, add the butter or margarine and rub in until the mixture resembles fine bread crumbs. Stir in the sugar. Add just enough cold water, 1 tbsp at a time, to mix to a soft dough. Gather into a ball and transfer to a lightly floured work surface. Knead the dough for several minutes or until soft and pliable.

Roll out the dough until about ⅛–¼ inch thick, then cut into 3 inch squares or rounds. Place a large tsp of the filling in the center of each piece of pastry.

If you have cut rounds, gather the edges together over the filling, pinch to close and roll into balls, or fold the pastry over to form half moons and seal the edges with the tines of a fork. If you have cut squares of pastry, fold into rectangles over the filling and seal with the tines of a fork.

Arrange on lightly greased baking sheets, brush the tops with beaten egg and sprinkle with sesame seeds. Bake for 30–40 minutes or until golden. Remove and cool on wire racks.

Almond and Pistachio-Filled Lover's Pastries

YESIL FISTIKLI KURABIYE

This is a Turkish version of Ghorayebah from the town of Gaziantep in the southern part of the country bordering Syria. Extra almonds or shredded dried coconut can be used instead of the pistachio nuts if you wish.

MAKES ABOUT 30

3¼ cups all-purpose flour	*Filling*
1 cup Clarified Butter (page 123), melted	½ lb blanched almonds, roughly chopped (about 2 cups)
2 tbsp rosewater	½ lb shelled unsalted pistachio nuts, roughly chopped (about 1⅓ cups)
5 tbsp milk	½ cup sugar
confectioners' sugar, to finish	1½ tsp ground cinnamon

Preheat the oven to 300°F.

First prepare the filling by mixing all the ingredients together in a bowl. Set aside.

Sift the flour into a large bowl and make a well in the center. Pour in the butter and mix by hand. Add the rosewater and milk and knead for several minutes until the dough is soft and pliable.

Break off walnut-sized lumps of dough and roll into balls. Take one ball and hollow it out with your thumb, pinching the sides up until they are thin and form a pot-shape. Spoon in some of the filling, then press the dough back over it to enclose it completely. Roll back into a ball, then press gently between your palms to flatten slightly.

Arrange the pastries on ungreased baking sheets and bake for about 20 minutes. Do not let them change color or the pastry will harden. Remove from the oven and leave to cool on wire racks.

Sift a generous amount of confectioners' sugar onto a large plate and roll the pastries in it. Store in an airtight tin.

"*Gazelle Horn*" Pastries filled with Almonds

TCHARAK

MAKES 16

1⅔ cups all-purpose flour	*Filling*
2 tbsp butter, melted	2⅔ cups ground almonds
3 tbsp orange blossom water	1½ cups confectioners' sugar, sifted
To finish	1 tsp ground cinnamon
orange blossom water	2–4 tbsp orange blossom water
about 1 cup confectioners' sugar	

Prepare the filling by mixing the almonds, confectioners' sugar and cinnamon together in a bowl. Add enough of the orange blossom water to bind the ingredients together. Knead until smooth and pliable. Divide into 16 balls and roll each one into a sausage, about 2 inches long, which is thicker in the middle and tapers at each end. Set aside.

Preheat the oven to 350°F.

Sift the flour into a large bowl, make a well in the center and add the melted butter and orange blossom water. Gradually work the flour into the liquid and, 1 tbsp at a time, add just enough cold water to form a dough. Transfer to a work surface and knead for about 20 minutes or until the dough is very smooth and elastic. Divide into two equal portions.

Take one portion of dough and roll it out into a strip about 4 inches wide and at least 30 inches long. You will find that you will be able to stretch the dough by wrapping first one end and then the other end over the rolling pin and pulling gently.

Arrange eight of the almond sausages on the pastry end to end in a line about 1½ inches in from the long edge nearest you, leaving about 2 inches between each sausage. Fold the long edge of the pastry over the sausages to enclose them completely. Cut down between each sausage.

Taking one pastry at a time, press the edges together to seal in the filling. Trim the long edge to a semicircle, but do not cut too close to the filling or the edges will be forced open during cooking. Crimp the edges with the tines of a fork. Now pinch the pastry and filling up to form a steep ridge and gently curve the ends around to form a crescent-shape. Repeat with the remaining pastries.

Repeat with the second portion of dough and remaining almond filling.

Arrange the pastries on greased baking sheets and bake for 20–30 minutes or until a pale golden.

Meanwhile pour some orange blossom water into a shallow bowl and sift the confectioners' sugar into another shallow bowl. When the pastries are cooked, remove them from the oven and, one at a time, soak them in the orange blossom water and then toss in the confectioners' sugar until completely coated and snow-white. Cool on wire racks, then store in an airtight tin. Dust with a little more confectioners' sugar before serving.

Lover's Pastries

GHORAYEBAH

"Wheat makes cakes, but bread satisfies hunger." – Greek saying

*T*he Middle Eastern cuisine is rich in pastries which are prepared with flour, semolina and sometimes baklava dough. They are often filled with nuts and/or fruits. Though sometimes fried, these pastries are more often baked and then stored in airtight containers. The most famed pastry, which appears throughout North Africa, the Middle East, the Balkans and as far as India, is Ghorayebah, a shortbread cookie that literally melts in the mouth. This classic version is from Northern Syria.

MAKES 18–20

2 sticks (8 oz) unsalted butter
1 cup confectioners' sugar, sifted
1⅔ cups all-purpose flour, sifted
about 10 blanched almonds, split

Melt the butter in a small saucepan over a low heat. Spoon off any froth and pour the yellow liquid into a large mixing bowl. Discard any white residue at the bottom of the pan. Refrigerate until the butter has solidified.

Preheat the oven to 300°F.

Remove the butter from the refrigerator and beat or whisk for several minutes until the butter is creamy and white. Add the confectioners' sugar, a little at a time, and continue to beat until smooth. Sift in the flour, a little at a time, and continue to mix until the dough becomes stiff. Gather up the dough and knead by hand until it becomes pliable. Set aside to rest for about 10 minutes.

Break off walnut-sized lumps of dough and roll each one into a thin sausage. Join the ends to form a circle and press an almond half over the seam. Continue until you have used up all the dough, placing the circles on ungreased baking sheets about 1 inch apart.

Bake for about 15 minutes or until the almonds are a very pale golden, but the cookies are still white. Do not let the cookies change color because it will alter their texture and flavor. Leave on the baking sheets for 1 minute, then transfer to a wire rack and leave until cold. Store in an airtight tin.

Illustrated on page 54

Greek-Style Shortbread with Ouzo

—————— KOURABITHES ——————

The classic Arab recipe for Ghorayebah passed to the Turks as Kurabiye and to the Greeks as Kourabithes. With the Greeks it took on religious connotations, for traditionally these pastries were prepared for Christmas and New Year's Day. There is a charming custom in Crete where a clove is stuck into each shortbread to symbolize the three Wise Men who brought the Mother of Christ spices and incense on that cold night in Bethlehem.

MAKES ABOUT 20

2 sticks (8 oz) unsalted butter
3 tbsp confectioners' sugar, sifted
1 egg yolk
1 tbsp ouzo or brandy
½ cup toasted and very finely chopped almonds
2 cups all-purpose flour, sifted
1 tsp baking powder
whole cloves
1½ cups confectioners' sugar, to finish

Melt the butter in a small saucepan over a low heat. Spoon off any froth and pour the yellow liquid into a large mixing bowl. Discard any white residue at the bottom of the pan. Refrigerate until the butter has solidified.

Preheat the oven to 325°F.

Whisk or beat the butter for several minutes until soft and white. Add the 3 tbsp of confectioners' sugar and beat in thoroughly, then add the egg yolk and ouzo or brandy and beat well. Stir in the chopped almonds, flour and baking powder. When the mixture becomes stiff, gather it into a ball and knead for several minutes until soft and pliable.

Break off walnut-sized lumps of dough and roll into balls. Flatten each one slightly, then pinch the top twice making four indentations. Press a clove into the top of each and place on ungreased baking sheets.

Bake for 15–20 minutes or until lightly golden. Do not let them brown or the flavor will change. Leave on the baking sheets to cool for 10 minutes.

Sift some of the confectioners' sugar over wax paper and place the warm Kourabithes on it. Sift more confectioners' sugar generously over them. When they are completely cold, store in an airtight container, sprinkling any remaining sugar over the top.

Illustrated on page 55

Lover's Pastries

Greek-Style Shortbread with Ouzo

$\mathscr{P}$istachio-Filled Pastries with Natife Cream

──── KARABIJ BIL NATIFE ────

*N*atife is the Syrian–Arabic name for bois de Panama, which is also sometimes called "halva wood" because it is used in the commercial sugar and sesame seed-based Halvas. Karabij is a small semolina-based pastry filled with walnuts or pistachios. There is nothing spectacular about the pastry, but the cream is out of this world – a unique experience! Bois de Panama is not the easiest ingredient to find, but good Middle Eastern food stores stock it and some health food shops will order it for you.

MAKES ABOUT 30

3¼ cups all-purpose flour	*Cream*
2 sticks (8 oz) unsalted butter, Wmelted	3 oz *bois de Panama*
	1 cup + 2 tbsp water
about 4 tbsp cold water	1 cup + 2 tbsp sugar
	1 tbsp lemon juice
	2 tbsp orange blossom water
	4 egg whites
	Filling
	½ lb shelled unsalted pistachios, finely chopped (about 1⅓ cups)
	½ cup sugar
	1½ tsp ground cinnamon

First prepare the cream. Pulverize the pieces of wood, place the powder in a bowl with ¾ cup of the water and leave to soak for 4–5 hours. Transfer the contents of the bowl to a saucepan and bring to a boil. Lower the heat and simmer until the liquid has thickened. Strain through fine cheesecloth or a dish towel and set the liquid aside.

Dissolve the sugar in the remaining water in a small saucepan, add the lemon juice and bring to a boil. Lower the heat and simmer for about 10 minutes or until the syrup has thickened. Remove from the heat, stir in the orange blossom water and the hot *bois de Panama* liquid and beat vigorously. Set aside to cool completely.

Place the egg whites in a large bowl and beat until very stiff. Gradually add the cold syrup mixture, beating constantly, until the mixture froths and expands. Transfer to a serving dish and set aside.

Mix the filling ingredients together.

Preheat the oven to 300°F.

To prepare the dough, sift the flour into a large bowl and make a well in the center. Pour in the butter and mix in with your fingertips. Add the cold water and knead until the dough is soft and pliable. Divide into walnut-sized lumps.

Taking one lump at a time, roll it into a ball and then hollow it out with your thumb, pinching the sides up until they are thin and form a pot-shape. Fill the center with a little of the nut filling and then press the dough back over it to enclose the filling and form a ball. Gently press between your palms to make an oval shape. Repeat until all the dough and filling have been used.

Place on baking sheets and bake for about 20 minutes. Remove from the oven before the pastry changes color – it should still be white. Transfer to wire racks and leave to cool.

To serve, arrange the Karabij on a large plate and offer with the bowl of natife cream. Dip the Karabij into the cream and eat. The pastries will keep for a long time in an airtight tin, but it is best to refrigerate the cream in a covered container.

Moroccan Semolina Pastry Balls

GHORIBA MUGHRABI

Yet another version of Ghorayebah, this time made with fine semolina.

MAKES ABOUT 25

2 sticks (8 oz) unsalted butter
1 cup confectioners' sugar, sifted
2⅓ cups semolina flour
confectioners' sugar, to finish

Melt the butter in a small saucepan over a low heat. Remove any froth from the surface and pour the yellow liquid into a large mixing bowl. Discard any white residue at the bottom of the pan. Add the confectioners' sugar and semolina flour and mix until stiff. Gather up and knead by hand for several minutes until smooth and pliable. Set aside to rest for 2–3 hours.

Preheat the oven to 350°F.

Knead the dough again until soft, then break off a walnut-sized lump. Pass it from one hand to the other until it becomes very soft. Place on a buttered baking sheet. Repeat until you have used up all the dough.

Bake for 10–15 minutes or until golden. Remove and leave to cool on the baking sheet.

When cold, sift a generous amount of confectioners' sugar over the pastries and store in an airtight tin.

$\mathcal{C}$ypriot Nut-Filled Lover's Pastries

—————— LOKUMIA PARAYEMISTA ——————

A *simpler version of ma-moul, you can substitute all-purpose flour for semolina flour if you wish.*

MAKES 18

2 sticks (8 oz) unsalted butter	*Filling*
3¼ cups semolina flour	1½ cups coarsely chopped blanched
2 inch piece cinnamon stick	almonds
1 cup water	¼ cup sugar
1 tbsp orange blossom water	1½ tsp ground cinnamon
	To finish
	¼ cup orange blossom water
	confectioners' sugar

Melt the butter in a small saucepan over a low heat. Remove any froth from the surface, then pour the yellow liquid into a large mixing bowl. Discard any white residue at the bottom of the pan. Pour the semolina flour into the bowl and mix in until the mixture resembles fine bread crumbs. Cover and leave for 6–8 hours or overnight.

Preheat the oven to 375°F.

To make the filling, mix together the nuts, sugar and cinnamon. Set aside.

Place the cinnamon stick and water in a small saucepan and bring to a boil. Discard the cinnamon stick and pour the water into the semolina mixture together with the orange blossom water. Mix until well blended. When cool enough to handle, gather the dough into a ball and knead until smooth and soft.

Divide the dough into 18 lumps. Taking one at a time, mold into oval shapes. Make a hole through the center from one end and then enlarge it by turning the dough in one hand and working the finger around inside it. Fill the hole with a little of the nut filling and then close the dough back over the filling. Roll between your palms to reform the oval shape. Place on an ungreased baking sheet and continue until you have used up all the ingredients.

Bake for about 20 minutes or until lightly golden. Remove from the oven and, while still hot, brush with orange blossom water. Sift confectioners' sugar generously over a sheet of wax paper and place the hot pastries on it. Sift more sugar over them until the pastries are thickly coated. Store in an airtight container when completely cold.

Serve with another dusting of confectioners' sugar.

$\mathcal{S}$*yrian Semolina Pastries filled with Dates and Nuts*

—————————— MA-MOUL ——————————

$\mathcal{T}$raditionally these pastries are pressed into a specially-made mold to give them a distinctive appearance, and are baked for Easter. The pastry is made with semolina flour, but if unavailable use all-purpose flour. The contrast between the crumbly "melt-in-the-mouth" pastry and the chewy date and nut filling is delicious.

MAKES ABOUT 30

3¼ cups semolina flour	*Filling*
2 sticks (8 oz) unsalted butter, melted	10 oz dates, pitted and roughly chopped (about 1⅔ cups)
3 tbsp rosewater	
¼ cup milk	⅔ cup water
confectioners' sugar, to finish	2½ cups coarsely chopped walnuts
	½ cup sugar
	1½ tsp ground cinnamon

Preheat the oven to 300°F.

First prepare the filling by placing the dates in a small pan with the water, nuts, sugar and cinnamon. Cook over a low heat, stirring constantly, until the dates are soft and the water has been absorbed. Remove from the heat and set aside to cool.

Pour the semolina flour into a large bowl and mix in the melted butter. Add the rosewater and milk and knead by hand until the dough is soft and pliable. Divide the dough into walnut-sized lumps and roll each into a ball. Take one ball and hollow it out with your thumb, pinching up the sides until they are thin and form a pot-shape. Spoon in some of the date and nut mixture, then press the dough back over the filling to enclose it completely. Roll back into a ball shape and then either press it between your palms to flatten slightly or, if you have a wooden spoon with a deep, curved bowl, mold each pastry with that. Repeat until you have used up all the ingredients.

Arrange the pastries on ungreased baking sheets and make decorative patterns across the top of each with the tines of a fork. The traditional pattern is to mark straight lines down the center.

Bake for about 20 minutes and take care not to let the pastries change color because the texture and flavor will change. Remove from the oven and cool on wire racks.

Sift a generous amount of confectioners' sugar onto a large plate and roll the cold pastries in it to coat thoroughly. Store in an airtight tin.

Armenian Date and Walnut Pastries

—————— ARMAVOV KATAH ——————

There are, apparently, over 150 types of date, and countries such as Tunisia, Iraq and Iran are abundantly rich in this dessert fruit. Consequently the Middle Eastern repertoire is full of date-based dishes and pastries. The recipe here is a typical example and it appears in one form or another throughout the region. These pastries will keep well and are marvelous with tea and coffee.

MAKES ABOUT 35

2 sticks (8 oz) butter	*Filling*
¼ cup sugar	4 tbsp butter
1 egg, beaten	½ lb pitted dates, chopped
½ cup milk	(about 1⅓ cups)
3¼ cups all-purpose flour	¼ cup milk
2 tsp baking powder	1 cup chopped walnuts
1 egg, beaten, to glaze	2 tbsp rosewater
	1½–2 tsp ground cinnamon

First prepare the filling: melt the butter in a small pan. Add the dates and milk and cook over a low heat, mashing frequently with a wooden spoon, until the dates form a soft pulp. Remove from the heat and stir in the remaining filling ingredients. Set aside to cool.

Preheat the oven to 350°F.

To make the dough, place the butter and sugar in a large bowl and beat until soft and creamy. Stir in the egg and milk. Sift in the flour and baking powder, a little at a time, stirring constantly until a soft dough is formed. Knead for a few minutes until smooth and pliable. Divide into two equal balls.

Divide the filling into six equal portions.

Lightly flour the work surface. Take one ball of dough and roll it out into a round about ⅛ inch thick. Arrange one portion of the filling in a ridge over the dough near the edge of the round closest to you. Roll over twice and then cut off from the remaining pastry so that you have a sausage filled with dates.

Arrange another ridge of the filling along the cut edge and roll up to form another sausage. Cut off from the remaining pastry. Arrange another ridge of the filling along the cut edge and then roll up to form another sausage.

Repeat with the remaining ball of dough and portions of filling.

Cut each prepared sausage across into 1–1½ inch pieces. Place them, 1 inch apart, on greased baking sheets. Glaze with the beaten egg, then bake for 20–30 minutes or until golden. Remove and cool on wire racks.

Illustrated on page 62

$\mathscr{A}$lgerian Lover's Pastries filled with Dates

—————— BRADJ ——————

*T*hese Berber pastries are traditionally cooked in a tajine – a shallow earthenware dish with a pointed lid – but excellent results can be obtained using a large skillet.

MAKES ABOUT 30

3¼ cups medium or fine semolina flour	*Filling*
1½ sticks (6 oz) unsalted butter, melted	½ lb dates, pitted and chopped (about 1⅓ cups)
2 tbsp orange blossom water	½ tsp ground cinnamon
½ cup water	pinch of ground cloves
melted butter for frying	

First prepare the filling: place the dates in a small saucepan with the cinnamon, cloves and a few tbsp of water. Cook over a low heat, mashing with a wooden spoon, until the mixture resembles a purée and the water has been absorbed. Shape into a ball and set aside to cool.

Place the semolina flour in a large bowl and make a well in the middle. Pour in the melted butter and rub in with your fingertips until all the semolina grains are coated with butter. Add the orange blossom water and just enough of the water to bind the mixture together. Knead until smooth.

Divide the dough into two equal parts. Take one and place it on the work surface. Place the ball of dates on top and then cover with the second ball of dough. Now gently flatten until you have a round, flat cake about ½ inch thick. Cut into 1 inch squares or lozenges.

Brush a skillet with a little melted butter, then arrange as many pastries in it as possible. Cover and cook over a low heat for about 20 minutes, turning once, until both sides are golden. Remove and place on a wire rack to cool while you cook any remaining pastries in the same way, brushing the pan with a little more butter first.

Illustrated on page 63

Armenian Date and Walnut Pastries

Algerian Lover's Pastries filled with Dates

Prune-Filled Sweet Pastries

—————————— SALORI BOREK ——————————

*D*elicious pastries, these can be served either as a dessert or with coffee or tea. Dried apricots make a tasty alternative to prunes if you prefer, and you can vary the nuts used in the filling.

MAKES 20

1⅔ cups all-purpose flour	*Filling*
1 stick butter, cut into small pieces	½ lb pitted prunes
	2 thin orange slices
3 egg yolks	¼ cup chopped walnuts
2–3 tbsp plain yoghurt	grated zest of 1 lemon
confectioners' sugar, to finish	juice of ½ lemon
	¼ cup sugar
	3 tbsp raisins
	½ tsp ground cinnamon

First prepare the filling: place the prunes and orange slices in a saucepan with just enough water to cover and simmer gently until the prunes are tender and the water has been absorbed. When cool enough to handle, chop the prunes and orange slices and place in a small bowl. Stir in the remaining filling ingredients and set aside until cold.

Sift the flour into a large bowl, add the pieces of butter and rub in until the mixture resembles fine bread crumbs. Beat the egg yolks in a small bowl with 2 tbsp of the yoghurt. Pour into the flour mixture and knead until a dough is formed. Add the remaining yoghurt if the dough is a little stiff. Transfer to a work surface and knead for several minutes or until smooth and soft.

Divide the dough into 20 balls. Arrange on a large plate, cover with a clean dish towel and refrigerate for 20–30 minutes.

Preheat the oven to 400°F.

Lightly flour a work surface. Take one of the balls of dough and roll it out to form a round about 3 inches in diameter. Repeat with all the remaining balls.

Put 1–2 teaspoons of the filling on one half of each round, then fold over and pleat the edges with your fingers or seal with a fork. Place on lightly greased baking sheets and bake for 20–30 minutes or until golden.

Remove from the oven and leave to cool a little. Serve warm or cold with a dusting of confectioners' sugar.

Quince-Filled Sweet Borek

SERGEVILOV BOREK

Quinces make a delicious filling for sweet borek, but apples can be used with equal success. These pastries can be served warm or cold, either as a dessert with cream or with tea or coffee.

MAKES 20

1⅔ cups all-purpose flour	*Filling*
1 stick butter, cut into small pieces	4 quinces, peeled, cored and finely chopped
3 egg yolks	2 tbsp chopped unsalted pistachio
2–3 tbsp plain yoghurt	nuts or hazelnuts (filberts)
½ cup confectioners' sugar, to finish	½ tsp ground cinnamon
	¼ cup sugar

Sift the flour into a large bowl, add the pieces of butter and rub in until the mixture resembles fine bread crumbs. Beat the egg yolks in a small bowl with 2 tbsp of the yoghurt. Pour into the flour mixture and knead until a dough is formed. Add the remaining yoghurt if the dough is stiff. Transfer to a work surface and knead for several minutes or until smooth and soft.

Divide the dough into 20 balls. Arrange on a large plate, cover with a dish towel and refrigerate for 20–30 minutes.

Preheat the oven to 400°F.

Place the filling ingredients in a small bowl and mix well.

Lightly flour a work surface. Take one of the balls of dough and roll it out to form a round about 3 inches in diameter. Repeat with all the remaining balls.

Put 1–2 teaspoons of the filling on one half of each round, then fold over and pleat the edges with your fingers or seal with a fork. Place on lightly greased baking sheets and bake for 20–30 minutes or until golden.

Remove from the oven and cool a little, then sprinkle with the confectioners' sugar.

Sweet Borek with Nut Filling

KHORITZ BOREK

Borek are either savory or sweet pastries which are filled with a great variety of mixtures and then baked or deep-fried. They are made with a special dough, but baklava filo pastry is sometimes used instead. You can vary the nuts used in the filling to your heart's content! Serve these pastries warm or cold, as a dessert or with tea or coffee.

MAKES 20

1⅔ cups all-purpose flour	*Filling*
1 stick butter, cut into small pieces	3 egg whites
	1 tsp almond extract
3 egg yolks	2 tbsp confectioners' sugar
2–3 tbsp plain yoghurt	½ lb (about 2 cups) mixed chopped nuts, such as unsalted almonds, pistachios and walnuts
	Topping
	½ cup confectioners' sugar
	½ tsp ground cinnamon
	½ tsp ground cardamom

Sift the flour into a large bowl, add the pieces of butter and rub in until the mixture resembles fine bread crumbs. Beat the egg yolks in a small bowl with 2 tbsp of the yoghurt. Pour into the flour mixture and knead until a dough is formed. Add the remaining yoghurt if the dough is stiff. Transfer to a work surface and knead for several minutes or until smooth and soft.

Divide the dough into 20 balls. Arrange on a large plate, cover with a clean dish towel and refrigerate for 20–30 minutes.

To prepare the filling, beat the egg whites together in a bowl until frothy, then stir in the remaining filling ingredients until evenly blended.

Preheat the oven to 400°F.

Lightly flour a work surface. Take one of the balls of dough and roll it out to form a round about 3 inches in diameter. Repeat with all the remaining balls.

Put 1–2 teaspoons of the filling on one half of each round, then fold over and pleat the edges with your fingers or seal with a fork. Place on lightly greased baking sheets and bake for 20–30 minutes or until golden.

Sift the topping ingredients together into a small bowl. When the Borek are cooked remove from the oven, leave to cool a little and then sprinkle with the topping mixture.

$\mathcal{T}$raditional Arab Sweet Borek filled with Dates

SAMBUSIK

"If Heaven drops a date, you must open your mouth." – Yiddish saying

*T*his is an ancient pastry from the days of Harun-el-Rashid, the Caliph of Baghdad, whose court
poet, Mahmud-ibn al-Hasain Kushajim, praised the virtues of Sambusik to the high heavens.
From Baghdad Sambusik was passed on to Northern India where today it is known as samosa.
Mahleb (page 8) gives the pastry its distinctive aroma and flavor.

MAKES 15–20

6 tbsp milk	*Filling*
¼ cup sugar	½ lb pitted dates, chopped (about
2 cups all-purpose flour	1⅓ cups)
½ tsp ground mahleb	4 tbsp butter
3 tbsp butter, melted	1 tbsp rosewater
¼ cup oil	
oil for deep-frying	
confectioners' sugar, to finish	

To prepare the filling, put the dates and butter in a small pan and cook over a medium heat, stirring
constantly, until the mixture is thick and soft. Remove from the heat, stir in the rosewater and set the
mixture aside to cool.

To make the dough, heat the milk and sugar in a small pan until the sugar has dissolved, then cool to
lukewarm. Sift the flour into a large bowl and add the mahleb and butter. Rub into the flour, then add the
sugared milk and oil. Mix until a soft dough is formed. Transfer to a work surface and knead for several
minutes or until smooth and pliable.

Lightly flour the work surface and roll out the dough until it is about ¼ inch thick. Cut into 3 inch rounds
with a plain cookie cutter. Place 1 tsp of the filling on one half of each round. Dampen the edges and fold
over. Crimp the edges with your fingers or seal with the tines of a fork.

Heat sufficient oil in a large saucepan to deep-fry to 350°F, then fry three or four Sambusik at a time for
several minutes, turning once, until golden and cooked through. Drain on paper towels. Serve warm or cold
with a generous sprinkling of sifted confectioners' sugar.

Cakes & Gatas

Gata with Sweet Filling

STEPANAVANI GATA

*A*ll the diverse cuisines of the Middle East and North Africa lack the richly decorated cakes and *gâteaux of Europe or the USA. Instead the Middle Easterners, in their pursuit of gratification, have developed dry cakes which are usually prepared with a sweet yeast mixture and often have fillings of nuts, fresh or dried fruits and spices. The tops of the cakes are often decorated with nuts or patterns. "Gata" is the name given to this type of cake in Armenia.*
This cake is a specialty of Stepanavan in Armenia. It has a simple sugar-butter filling.

MAKES 3 CAKES

½ oz compressed yeast, or	**Filling**
1 package active dry yeast	1 stick butter
1 cup lukewarm milk	¾ cup all-purpose flour
¼ cup sugar	4–6 tbsp sugar
10 tbsp butter, melted	
2⅔ cups all-purpose flour	
½ tsp salt	
1 egg, beaten, to glaze	

Place the yeast in a small bowl with half the milk. If compressed yeast, cream together; if dry, stir to dissolve.

Pour the remaining milk into a large bowl, add the sugar and stir until it has dissolved, then stir in 8 tbsp (½ cup) of the melted butter. Stir in the yeast mixture, then sift in the flour and salt and mix until a dough is formed. Gather it into a ball and transfer to a lightly floured work surface. Knead for at least 10 minutes or until smooth and elastic.

Roll the dough into a ball, place in a clean bowl, cover with a dish towel and set aside in a warm place to rise for at least 2 hours or until doubled in bulk.

Prepare the filling: melt the butter in a small pan, add the flour and fry, stirring constantly, until golden. Stir in the sugar and set aside.

Transfer the risen dough to a work surface, punch down and knead for a few more minutes. Divide into three equal parts. Lightly flour the work surface. Take one portion of dough and roll it out until ⅛–¼ inch thick. Brush the surface all over with a little of the remaining melted butter, then fold the edges into the center to make a 5 inch square.

Place one-third of the filling in the center of the square and bring the opposite corners of the square over to enclose the filling completely. Carefully roll out the cake until it is about 6 inches square. Do not let the filling ooze out. Place on a greased baking sheet. Repeat with the remaining dough and filling.

Brush the top of each gata with beaten egg, then set aside in a warm place to rise for a further 30 minutes. Preheat the oven to 400°F.

Bake for about 20 minutes or until risen and golden. Remove and cool on wire racks. Serve sliced.

Greek New Year's Cake

—————— VASILOPITA ——————

St Basil's cake is made specially for New Year's Day and it is served just after the Old Year's departure. Traditionally a gold coin is inserted into the dough and whoever finds it is considered to be the lucky person of the New Year. It is advisable to wrap the coin in a little foil first.

MAKES 1 LARGE CAKE

2⅓ cups all-purpose flour
2 tsp baking powder
2 sticks (8 oz) unsalted butter, softened
1 cup + 2 tbsp sugar
4 eggs
1 cup fresh orange juice
1 tbsp aniseed
⅓ cup sesame seeds
about 1 cup blanched almonds, to garnish

Preheat the oven to 350°F. Lightly grease and flour a baking pan, about 8 × 12 × 2 inches.

Sift the flour and baking powder into a bowl and set aside.

Place the butter and sugar in a large bowl and beat until light and creamy. One at a time, beat in the eggs. Using a metal spoon, gradually stir in one-third of the flour and then one-third of the orange juice. Repeat with the remaining flour and juice. Add the aniseed and sesame seeds and mix thoroughly. Drop in the coin.

Pour the batter into the baking pan and smooth over the surface with the back of a spoon. Write the New Year's date on the top of the cake with the blanched almonds, or use them to create a decorative pattern.

Bake in the center of the oven for 50–60 minutes or until risen and golden. Unmold onto a wire rack and, when cold, cut into square or lozenge shapes.

Illustrated on page 74

Jewish Purim Festival Cake with Nut and Jam Filling

—— PURIM STOLLEN ——

Purim is the Feast of Lots which originated about 2,400 years ago in Persia. Purim signifies celebration and during the Feast many sweet desserts and cakes are prepared. A classic is this recipe below with a jam and nut filling.

MAKES 10–12 SLICES

1 egg, beaten	*Filling*
5 tbsp evaporated milk	grated zest of 1 lemon
½ cup sugar	2 tbsp lemon juice
1⅓ cups fine graham cracker crumbs	2 tbsp sugar
1⅔ cups all-purpose flour, sifted	⅓ cup apricot jam or other jam of
4 tbsp butter, melted	your choice
	3 tbsp chopped hazelnuts (filberts) or walnuts
	⅓ cup poppy seeds

Preheat the oven to 400°F.

Place all the filling ingredients in a bowl and mix thoroughly. Set aside.

To make the dough, put the egg, milk, sugar, cracker crumbs, flour and 3 tbsp of the melted butter into a large bowl and mix thoroughly to form a stiff dough. Gather up into a ball and transfer to a lightly floured work surface. Knead for several minutes or until pliable.

Roll out the dough into a rectangle about 10 × 15 inches. Brush the surface all over with some of the melted butter.

Arrange the filling down one of the long sides of the rectangle about 1 inch in from the edge. Spread it out a little so that one half of the rectangle is covered. Carefully fold the pastry over the filling and pinch the edges together so that the filling is completely sealed in.

Lift gently onto a large, greased baking sheet. Brush the stollen all over with any remaining melted butter and bake for 20–25 minutes or until a golden brown.

Remove from the oven and leave to cool a little, then cut into diagonal slices. Serve warm.

Easter Cake with Dried Fruits and Nut Filling

ZADGVA GATA

MAKES 3 CAKES

½ oz compressed yeast, or	*Filling*
1 package active dry yeast	2 tbsp butter
1 cup lukewarm milk	2 tbsp raisins
¼ cup sugar	2 tbsp chopped walnuts
1 stick unsalted butter, melted	1 tbsp brown sugar
2⅔ cups all-purpose flour	1 tbsp sugar
½ tsp salt	1 tsp ground cinnamon
	1 tbsp sesame seeds
	To finish
	2 tbsp butter, melted
	1 egg, beaten

Place the yeast in a small bowl with half the milk. If compressed yeast, cream together; if dry, stir to dissolve.

Pour the remaining milk into a large bowl, add the sugar and stir until dissolved. Add the yeast mixture and butter and stir well. Sift in the flour and salt and mix until a dough is formed. Gather into a ball and transfer to a lightly floured work surface. Knead for at least 10 minutes or until soft and smooth.

Roll the dough into a ball, place in a clean bowl, cover with a dish towel and set aside in a warm place to rise for about 2 hours or until doubled in bulk.

To prepare the filling, melt the butter in a small pan and stir in all the remaining filling ingredients. Set aside.

When risen, punch down the dough, transfer to the work surface and knead for a few minutes. Divide the dough into three equal portions. Take one and roll it out on the floured work surface until about ⅛–¼ inch thick. Brush the surface thoroughly with the melted butter and then fold the edges into the center to form a 5 inch square. Place one-third of the filling in the center of the square and bring the opposite corners of the square over to enclose the filling completely. Gently roll out the cake until it is a 6 inch square, taking care not to let the filling ooze out. Place on a greased baking sheet. Repeat with the remaining dough and filling.

Brush the top of each cake with the beaten egg, then place the baking sheets in a warm place and leave to rise for 30 minutes.

Preheat the oven to 400°F.

Bake for about 20 minutes or until risen and golden. Remove and cool on wire racks.

Illustrated on page 75

Semolina, Cardamom and Almond Cake

ARTZAK GATA

MAKES 3 CAKES

½ oz compressed yeast, or	*Filling*
1 package active dry yeast	¾ cup Clarified Butter (page 123)
1 tsp + 6 tbsp sugar	¾ cup semolina flour
2 tbsp lukewarm water	1⅓ cups ground almonds
¼ cup Clarified Butter (page 123), melted	¼ tsp ground cardamom
	1¼ cups confectioners' sugar
2 eggs	*To finish*
⅔ cup milk	2 tbsp Clarified Butter (page 123), melted
½ tsp salt	
1 tsp vanilla extract	1 egg, beaten
½ tsp ground mastic (page 8)	
3¼ cups all-purpose flour	

Place the yeast in a small bowl with 1 tsp of the sugar and the water. If compressed yeast, cream together; if dry, stir to dissolve. Leave in a warm place for 15–20 minutes or until the mixture begins to froth.

Place the butter, eggs, milk, remaining sugar, salt, vanilla and mastic in a large bowl. Add the yeast mixture and stir well. Sift in the flour, stirring constantly, until a dough is formed. Gather up into a ball and transfer to a lightly floured work surface. Knead for about 10 minutes or until the dough is soft and elastic.

Place the dough in a clean bowl, cover with a dish towel and set aside in a warm place to rise for about 2 hours or until doubled in bulk.

To prepare the filling, first melt the butter in a saucepan, add the semolina and fry, stirring constantly, until the semolina is a pale gold. Add the remaining filling ingredients and cook for a further 2 minutes, stirring all the time. Set aside.

Preheat the oven to 350°F.

Punch down the dough and knead for a few minutes. Divide into three equal portions and roll into balls. Lightly flour a work surface. Take one ball of dough and roll it out into a round about ¼ inch thick. Brush the round with some of the melted butter and then spread one-third of the filling evenly over it to within ½ inch of the edge. Fold the dough in half to form a half moon and then carefully roll it out to make it a little larger and a round shape about ½ inch thick. Place on a greased baking sheet. Repeat with the remaining dough and filling.

Use your fingertips to press around the edge of each cake to give a fluted appearance. Make a pattern on the top of each with the tines of a fork and then brush with the beaten egg.

Bake for 30–40 minutes or until golden. Transfer to wire racks and leave until cold. Store in airtight tins.

Greek New Year's Cake

Easter Cake with Dried Fruits and Nut Filling

$\mathscr{M}$astic and Sugar Cake

──── SHAKAROV GATA ────

A *truly aromatic cake of delicate flavor, this is often eaten plain, but it is also delicious when spread with a little jam or honey.*

MAKES 6 CAKES

½ oz compressed yeast, or 1 package active dry yeast
1 tsp sugar
6 tbsp lukewarm water
1 cup confectioners' sugar
⅞ cup milk
4 tbsp butter, melted
2 tbsp olive oil
1 tsp salt
1 tsp mahleb (page 8), crushed
1 tsp poppy seeds
3¼ cups all-purpose flour, sifted
1 egg, beaten, to glaze

Place the yeast and sugar in a small bowl with the warm water. If compressed yeast, cream together; if dry, stir to dissolve. Leave in a warm place for 15–20 minutes or until the mixture begins to froth.

Sift the confectioners' sugar into a large bowl. Add the milk, butter, oil and yeast mixture and mix thoroughly. Add the salt, mahleb and poppy seeds and stir well. Gradually add the flour and mix to form a dough. Gather up into a ball and transfer to a lightly floured work surface. Knead for about 10 minutes or until smooth and pliable. (Alternatively, knead the dough using the dough hook in a heavy duty (countertop) electric mixer.)

Place the dough in a clean bowl, cover with a clean cloth and set aside in a warm place to rise for about 2 hours or until doubled in bulk.

Transfer the dough to a lightly floured work surface, punch down and knead for a few minutes. Divide the dough into six portions and roll each into a ball. Take one and roll it out into a round about ½ inch thick. Place on a greased baking sheet. Repeat with the remaining balls of dough.

Brush the tops with the beaten egg, then set aside in a warm place to rise for a further 30 minutes.

Preheat the oven to 350°F.

Bake for 25–30 minutes or until golden brown. Remove, cool on wire racks and when completely cold store in an airtight tin.

$\mathscr{S}$emolina and Yoghurt Cake soaked in Syrup

——— BASBOUSA-BIL-LABAN ———

One of the many semolina-based sweets to be found throughout the Middle East. It is delicious but rich, so serve in small pieces, with or without cream.

MAKES 12–14 PIECES

scant ½ cup blanched almonds	*Syrup*
⅔ cup plain yoghurt	1 cup + 2 tbsp sugar
2 sticks (8 oz) unsalted butter, melted	⅔ cup water
½ cup sugar	2 tbsp lemon juice
1¼ cups semolina flour	
1 tsp baking powder	
1 tsp vanilla extract	

Preheat the oven to 400°F. Grease and flour a round baking pan, about 8 inches in diameter.

Prepare the syrup by placing all the ingredients in a small pan and bringing slowly to a boil. Lower the heat and simmer for about 10 minutes or until the syrup forms a slightly sticky film on the back of a spoon. Set aside to cool.

Toast the almonds under the broiler until golden, turning once. Remove and chop finely.

Pour the yoghurt into a large mixing bowl and add half the melted butter, the sugar, semolina flour, baking powder, vanilla and chopped almonds. Mix thoroughly until well blended. Pour the batter into the cake pan and smooth over the surface with the back of a spoon.

Bake for about 30 minutes or until the surface of the cake is golden. Remove the Basbousa from the oven and pour the cold syrup evenly over it. Cut into lozenge shapes and return to the oven for a further 3–4 minutes.

Warm the remaining butter. Remove the Basbousa from the oven and pour the butter evenly over the surface. Leave to cool.

Israeli Orange and Walnut Cake

— UGAT TAPOUZ —

The famous "Shamouti" or "Jaffa" oranges of Israel are put to good use here when mixed with raisins and walnuts. This is a typical example of a new cuisine that is emerging in the Middle East, where the best of East and West are combined to create a very exciting school of cooking.

MAKES 1 LARGE CAKE

1 orange	*Topping*
⅔ cup currants	5 tbsp orange juice
2 oz (about ½ cup) shelled walnuts	1 tbsp lemon juice
1⅔ cups self-rising flour	¼ cup sugar
¼ tsp baking soda	1 tsp ground cinnamon
¾ cup sugar	
10 tbsp butter, softened	
1 cup milk	
2 eggs	

Preheat the oven to 350°F. Grease and flour a round cake pan about 7½ inches in diameter.

Cut the orange in half and squeeze out the juice. (Reserve the juice for the topping.) Cut the squeezed orange into pieces, place in a blender and reduce to a pulp. Scrape out into a bowl. Next blend the currants and then the walnuts. Add both to the bowl and mix thoroughly.

Sift the flour and soda into a large mixing bowl and stir in the sugar. Add the butter and ¾ cup of the milk and cream together until smooth and light. Add the eggs and remaining milk and beat for 1–2 minutes. Gently stir in the orange–nut mixture until evenly distributed.

Spoon into the cake pan and bake for 45–50 minutes or until a skewer inserted into the center comes out clean.

Mix the orange and lemon juices together. Remove the cake from the oven and immediately pour the juices evenly over the cake. Mix the sugar and cinnamon together and sprinkle over the surface. Set aside until cold.

Spiced Yoghurt Cake

— MADZNOUNOW GATA —

Yoghurt in its natural plain form is much used in desserts and pastries, particularly in Turkey and Armenia. This is a moist cake with a rich crunchy topping of coconut and walnuts.

MAKES 1 LARGE CAKE

1⅔ cups all-purpose flour	*Topping*
1½ tsp ground cinnamon	½ cup shredded dried coconut
½ tsp ground cloves	½ cup finely chopped walnuts
½ tsp grated nutmeg	¾ cup brown sugar
2 tsp baking powder	¼ cup heavy cream
½ tsp salt	6 tbsp Clarified Butter (page 123),
1 tsp baking soda	melted
3 large eggs	
1¾ cups brown sugar	
¾ cup Clarified Butter (page 123), melted	
1 cup plain yoghurt	

Preheat the oven to 325°F. Grease and flour a cake pan about 8½ inches in diameter.

Sift the flour, cinnamon, cloves, nutmeg, baking powder, salt and baking soda into a large mixing bowl. Make a well in the center. Break the eggs into a large bowl, add the sugar and whisk well. Stir in the melted butter and yoghurt. Pour this mixture into the flour and fold it in until well blended.

Spoon into the cake pan and smooth over the surface with the back of a spoon. Bake for 40–45 minutes or until a skewer inserted into the center comes out clean. Unmold onto a wire rack to cool.

Mix all the topping ingredients together in a bowl and spread evenly over the top of the cake when cool. Place the cake under a hot broiler for 2–3 minutes or until the topping is golden and crisp, but take care not to burn. Return to the wire rack until cold.

Jewish "Sabbath" Honey and Spice Cake

——— UGAT DVASH ———

This cake is served on the Sabbath, as its name suggests. The sweetness of the honey is contrasted with the pungency of the ginger and the aroma of the cloves. Serve cut into slices and spread with a little butter.

MAKES 1 LARGE CAKE

3 tbsp butter
⅔ cup clear honey
6 tbsp brown sugar
¼ cup milk
3 eggs
1 tsp baking soda, dissolved in 1 tbsp milk
2 cups all-purpose flour
1 tsp ground ginger
pinch of salt
1 tsp apple pie spice
¼ tsp ground cloves
½ cup sliced almonds

Preheat the oven to 350°F. Grease and flour a round cake pan, about 8 inches in diameter.

Place the butter, honey and sugar in a small saucepan and place over a low heat, stirring constantly until the sugar has dissolved. Set aside.

Place the milk, eggs and soda mixture in a bowl and whisk until frothy.

Sift the flour, ginger, salt, apple pie spice and cloves into a large bowl and make a well in the center. Pour in both the honey mixture and the egg and milk mixture. Using a metal spoon, mix both liquids together and gradually work in the flour. When it has all been absorbed and the mixture is smooth, pour into the cake pan. Smooth the surface over with the back of a spoon. Scatter the sliced almonds evenly over the top and press down gently into the surface.

Bake for about 1 hour or until a skewer inserted into the center comes out clean. Remove from the oven and leave to cool in the pan for about 30 minutes. Unmold onto a wire rack and leave until completely cold before serving.

Tea & Coffee Time

"Pretty Eyes" Cookies

— DILBER GOZU —

These cookies are not only visually stunning, they also taste delicious. They are a specialty of Istanbul and are marvelous with tea or coffee. Use any firmly-set jam of your choice.

MAKES 20–24

	To finish
2 sticks (8 oz) unsalted butter, at room temperature	thick jam
1 cup confectioners' sugar	confectioners' sugar
1 tsp vanilla extract	
2½ cups all-purpose flour, sifted	

Preheat the oven to 350°F.

Place the butter in a large bowl and beat until pale and creamy. Sift in the confectioners' sugar and add the vanilla, then continue to beat until smooth. Gradually stir in the flour and when the mixture becomes too stiff knead by hand until the dough is smooth. Divide the dough into two equal portions.

Lightly flour the work surface and roll out one portion of dough to ¼ inch thick. Using a 2 inch fluted cookie cutter, cut out as many rounds as possible; or cut into stars, crescents or other shapes. Repeat with the other portion of pastry.

Place half the cookies on lightly buttered baking sheets. Make three holes, about ¼–½ inch in diameter, in each of the remaining cookies. The clean top of a ball point pen (with its cap on) is ideal! Place on the baking sheets.

Bake for 10–15 minutes or until lightly golden. Transfer to wire racks and leave to cool.

Spread a little jam over the whole cookies. Place the cookies with holes on the work surface and sprinkle generously with sifted confectioners' sugar. Place these cookies over the ones with jam and press down gently so that the jam oozes up the holes. Store in an airtight tin.

Christian Festive Dry Crackers

———— CHOREG ————

There are several versions of these dry breads called choreg by the Turks and Armenians, tsoureki by the Greeks and Cypriots and kahk or simit in Arab lands. The name "choreg" comes from the Armenian chor meaning "dry" and eg (ekmeg) meaning "bread" in Turkish. This recipe makes use of mahleb. You can omit it, but the Choreg will lack one of its most distinctive characteristics. Serve the Choreg plain or with cheese or jam.

MAKES 25–30

½ oz compressed yeast, or	**To finish**
1 package active dry yeast	1 egg
1 tsp sugar	sesame seeds
1 cup lukewarm water	
3¼ cups all-purpose flour	
pinch of salt	
1 stick margarine or butter	
1 tsp mahleb (page 8), crushed	
½–1 cup cold water	
1 tbsp cooking oil	

Place the yeast, sugar and warm water in a small bowl. If compressed yeast, cream together; if dry, stir to dissolve. Set aside in a warm place for 15–20 minutes or until the mixture begins to froth.

Sift the flour and salt into a large bowl. Cut the margarine or butter into small pieces and add to the flour. Rub it in until the mixture resembles fine bread crumbs. Stir in the crushed mahleb. Make a well in the center and add the yeast mixture. Mix until you have a stiff dough. Now gradually blend in enough of the cold water, a little at a time, until you have a soft dough. The amount of water will depend a little on the absorbency of the flour.

Transfer to a floured work surface and knead for at least 10 minutes or until smooth and elastic. Add the oil and knead it in thoroughly.

Wash and dry the mixing bowl and lightly oil it. Add the ball of dough and roll it around the bowl to grease its surface. This will help prevent it from drying and cracking. Cover the bowl with a clean dish towel and leave in a warm place to rise for at least 2 hours or until the dough has doubled in bulk.

Preheat the oven to 400°F. Grease several baking sheets with cooking oil. Beat the egg in a small bowl and pour some sesame seeds onto a plate.

Punch down the dough and knead for a few minutes. Break off a piece about the size of a walnut and roll between your palms to form a ball. Place on a clean work surface and roll it to and fro with your palms to form a pencil-thin strip about 12 inches long. This strip can then be made into a variety of shapes. To make the twisted ring, bring one end of the strip over to meet the other, thus halving its original length.

Lightly roll your palm over the loose ends two or three times to form a twisted strip. Bring the two ends of the twisted strip together and press the uncut end over the loose ends to form a ring.

Place each Choreg, as you make it, on the greased baking sheets, leaving a little space between each one. Brush the tops with beaten egg and sprinkle with sesame seeds.

Turn the oven off, place the baking sheets inside and leave for 15–20 minutes or until the Choreg have risen a little. Turn the oven on again, to 400°F and bake for 12–15 minutes or until golden. As they are cooked, remove the Choreg from the oven and pile onto one large baking sheet. When they are all cooked, turn the oven off and return the tray of Choreg to it. Leave for several hours or until the crackers are cold and have dried out. Store in an airtight container.

Illustrated on page 86

Green Pistachio Cookies

——— YESIL FISTIK BISKUITI ———

MAKES 28

	Topping
1 stick butter, at room temperature	a little jam of your choice
¼ cup sugar	glacé cherries, halved
¼ tsp ground cinnamon	
finely grated zest of 1 lemon	
1 egg yolk	
¾ cup all-purpose flour	
¼ lb shelled unsalted green pistachio nuts, finely ground (about 1⅓ cups)	

Put the butter, sugar, cinnamon and lemon zest in a bowl and beat until creamy. Beat in the egg yolk. Sift the flour into the bowl, add the ground pistachio nuts and mix in with a metal spoon until thoroughly blended.

Transfer to a work surface and divide into two equal parts. Lightly dust the work surface with a little sifted flour or confectioners' sugar and roll each portion of dough into a sausage about 8 inches in length. Place on a baking sheet and refrigerate for 1 hour.

Preheat the oven to 350°F. Grease two large baking sheets.

Remove the dough from the refrigerator and cut each sausage into 14 equal pieces. Taking one at a time, roll between your palms and then flatten slightly until about 1½ inches in diameter. Arrange on the baking sheets about 1 inch apart. Make a slight hollow in the middle of each with your fingertip and place a little jam in it. Top with half a glacé cherry.

Bake for 10–15 minutes or until lightly golden. Remove, transfer to wire racks and leave until cold.

Illustrated on page 87

Christian Festive Dry Crackers

Green Pistachio Cookies

Damascene Dry Sesame Cookies

BERAZEH SHAMI

*O*ne *of the great specialties of the city of Damascus (Syria), these thin, round cookies are so popular they are exported throughout the Arab world. Marvelous with tea or coffee.*

MAKES ABOUT 24

½ oz compressed yeast, or	*Topping*
1 package active dry yeast	3 tbsp butter, melted
1 tsp + 1¾ cups sugar	1¼ cups sesame seeds
⅔ cup lukewarm water	
3¼ cups all-purpose flour	
1½ sticks (6 oz) butter, cut into small pieces	
3 tbsp coarsely chopped unsalted pistachio nuts	

Place the yeast, 1 tsp sugar and the warm water in a small bowl. If compressed yeast, cream together; if dry stir to dissolve. Set aside in a warm place for 15–20 minutes or until the mixture begins to froth.

Sift the flour into a large bowl and stir in the remaining sugar. Add the butter and rub in with your fingertips until the mixture resembles fine bread crumbs. Stir in the chopped nuts. Make a well in the center and add the yeast mixture. Mix until a dough is formed, adding a little more water if necessary.

Transfer to a work surface and knead for about 10 minutes or until soft and pliable. (Alternatively, knead the dough using the dough hook in a heavy duty (countertop) electric mixer.) Wash and dry the mixing bowl, add the dough and cover with a clean cloth. Set aside in a warm place to rise for about 2 hours.

Preheat the oven to 325°F.

Transfer the dough to a lightly floured work surface and knead for a few minutes. Divide into two portions. Keeping the work surface floured, roll out one portion until about ⅛ inch thick. Using a 4 inch cutter, cut out as many rounds as possible. Repeat with the remaining portion of dough.

Brush the surface of one round with a little melted butter and then place it, butter side down on the sesame seeds. Shake off the excess seeds and place the round on a greased baking sheet, seed side up. Repeat with the remaining cookies.

Bake for 15–20 minutes or until golden. Remove from the oven and transfer to wire racks. When completely cold, store in an airtight tin.

Illustrated on page 90

North African Raisin and Almond Cookies

FEQA'MIN ZBIB

MAKES 80–100

½ oz compressed yeast, or 1 package active dry yeast
1 tsp sugar
4–5 tbsp lukewarm water
2½ cups all-purpose flour
1 tsp salt
4 tbsp butter
1 cup confectioners' sugar
⅔ cup ground almonds
¼ cup orange blossom water
1 tbsp aniseed
⅓ cup raisins
½ tsp ground mastic (page 8)

Place the yeast, sugar and warm water in a small bowl. If compressed yeast, cream together; if dry, stir to dissolve. Set aside in a warm place for 15–20 minutes or until the mixture begins to froth.

Sift half the flour into a large bowl. Rub in the butter, then stir in the salt and yeast mixture. Gradually add just enough cold water to make a soft dough. Transfer to a lightly floured work surface and knead for about 10 minutes until smooth and elastic.

Wash and dry the bowl, add the dough and cover with a dish towel. Leave in a warm place to rise for at least 2 hours or until it has doubled in bulk.

Sift in the remaining flour and the confectioners' sugar and add all the remaining ingredients. Knead for several minutes until well blended.

Divide the dough into apple-sized lumps and roll into balls. Taking one at a time, roll into a sausage shape about 8 inches long and ½–¾ inch thick. Place well apart on greased baking sheets and set aside in a warm place to rise for a further 2 hours.

Preheat the oven to 350°F.

Prick the surface of each sausage in several places, then bake for 7–9 minutes or until half-cooked. Do not let them brown. Remove from the oven and leave for 5–6 hours or overnight.

Preheat the oven to 350°F.

Cut each sausage into 1 inch pieces and place on a large baking sheet. Bake until golden. Remove from the oven, cool on wire racks and store in an airtight tin.

Illustrated on page 91

Damascene Dry Sesame Cookies

North African Raisin and Almond Cookies
Iranian Cocoa and Lemon Cookies

$\mathcal{I}$ranian Cocoa and Lemon Cookies

NAN-E SHIRINI

$\mathcal{I}$ranians in general do not have pâtisserie, unlike the Arabs and Turks. They make great use of fruits – fresh or dried – and of confectionery prepared from rice flour and chickpea flour. This recipe, therefore, is an anomaly and a tasty one at that. It is a specialty of the fertile region of Shiraz.

MAKES 26–28

¾ cup Clarified Butter (page 123)	*Topping*
¾ cup sugar	1 egg white, beaten
1 egg yolk	2–3 tbsp finely chopped unsalted
1 tsp grated lemon zest	pistachio nuts
1⅔ cups all-purpose flour	
2 tbsp cocoa powder	

Place the butter in a large bowl and beat until light and creamy. Add the sugar, egg yolk and lemon zest and beat in until well blended. Sift in the flour and cocoa powder and knead until the mixture forms a smooth ball. Refrigerate for 1 hour.

Preheat the oven to 350°F.

Lightly flour the work surface. Divide the dough into half. Roll out one portion until about ¼ inch thick. Using a 2 inch fluted cookie cutter, cut out as many rounds as possible. Place on lightly greased baking sheets. Repeat with the remaining dough.

Brush the top of each cookie with a little beaten egg white and sprinkle with chopped pistachio nuts. Bake for about 15 minutes. Remove and cool on wire racks until cold. Store in an airtight tin.

Illustrated on page 91

Armenian Tahini and Walnut Balls

TAHINOV KUNTIG

These tasty little cookies were originally made especially for Lent.

MAKES ABOUT 20

4 tbsp butter, at room temperature
2 tbsp lard
½ cup tahini (page 8)
½ cup sugar
1 egg
1⅔ cups all-purpose flour
½ tsp baking powder
½ tsp baking soda
pinch of salt
½ cup finely chopped walnuts

Preheat the oven to 350°F.

Place the butter, lard, tahini and sugar in a large bowl and beat together until smooth. Add the egg and continue to beat until well blended. Sift the flour, baking powder, baking soda and salt into the bowl and fold into the creamed mixture. Add the nuts and mix until evenly distributed.

Break off walnut-sized lumps and roll into balls. Arrange about 2 inches apart on ungreased baking sheets and flatten slightly with the palm of your hand until they have a diameter of 1½ inches. Bake for about 15 minutes or until golden. Remove and cool on wire racks.

Lebanese Dry Cookies with Aniseed and Raisins

QIRSHALLI

These are tasty and aromatic cookies. The dough is first cooked whole, then cut into fingers and returned to the oven to dry out. This recipe uses semolina flour, but all-purpose flour can be used instead if you prefer.

MAKES ABOUT 30

2 cups semolina flour
2 tsp baking powder
½ cup vegetable oil
3 eggs
½ cup sugar
1 tsp vanilla extract
1½ tsp aniseed
⅓ cup raisins
½ cup chopped hazelnuts (filberts) or walnuts
1 egg yolk, beaten, to glaze

Sift the semolina flour and baking powder into a large bowl. Make a well in the center and add the oil. Rub in with your fingers until the mixture resembles fine bread crumbs. Place the eggs, sugar, vanilla and aniseed in another bowl and beat well. Pour into the flour mixture and mix in thoroughly. Stir in the raisins and nuts. Cover the bowl with a clean cloth and set aside to rest for about 15 minutes.

Preheat the oven to 350°F. Grease a baking pan, about 12 × 9 × 2 inches.

Spoon the mixture into the pan. Smooth over the surface with the back of a spoon and brush with the beaten egg yolk. Bake for 30 minutes.

Remove from the oven and leave to cool for 10 minutes, then unmold onto a work surface. Cut into fingers about 3 inches long and ½ inch wide. Pile the fingers onto a baking sheet.

Lower the oven temperature to 250°F. Return the cookies to the oven and bake for 20–30 minutes or until evenly browned. Remove from the oven and leave until cold.

Store in an airtight tin.

Moroccan Sesame Seed Cookies

──── GHORIBA DIAL JELJLANE ────

Sesame – whether seeds, powder or oil – is much used in the Middle East. This type of dry cookie is found all along the coast of North Africa and Southern Europe. These have the distinctive, earthy flavor characteristic of sesame.

MAKES ABOUT 20

½ lb (about 1⅔ cups) sesame seeds
¾ cup all-purpose flour, sifted
¾ cup sugar
1 tbsp baking powder
grated zest of 1 lemon
3 eggs
2 tsp vanilla extract
½ cup confectioners' sugar

Preheat the oven to 350°F.

Place the sesame seeds in a saucepan and cook over a medium heat, stirring constantly, until golden. Set aside to cool.

Place the flour in another pan and cook in the same way. Turn the flour into a large bowl.

Place the sesame seeds in a blender and reduce to a powder. Add this to the flour together with the sugar, baking powder and lemon zest. Make a well in the center and add the eggs and vanilla. Mix well, then knead for about 10 minutes or until the dough is smooth.

Oil your palms. Break off walnut-sized lumps of dough and roll into balls. Sift the confectioners' sugar onto a large plate. Take one ball at a time, press it into the sugar and flatten to a round about ½ inch thick. Arrange them on greased baking sheets about ½ inch apart with the sugar side up.

Bake for about 15 minutes or until lightly golden. Remove and cool on wire racks.

Cookies with Poppy Seeds

———— MOHN KICHLACH ————

Kichlachs are small crackers which go down well with cheese or as party snacks. Mohn kichlach are a sweeter version which incorporate poppy seeds.

MAKES 35–40

1 egg
½ cup sugar
6 tbsp butter, softened
3 tbsp poppy seeds
1⅔ cups all-purpose flour
2 tsp baking powder
½ tsp salt
2 tbsp water

Break the eggs into a large bowl and beat lightly. Add the sugar, butter and poppy seeds and beat until smooth and creamy. Sift in the flour, baking powder and salt and work into the mixture. Add enough of the water to form a soft dough. Transfer to a floured work surface and knead for several minutes or until smooth. Roll into a ball and refrigerate for about 1 hour.

Preheat the oven to 350°F.

Lightly flour the work surface and roll out the dough until about ⅛ inch thick. Using decorative cookie cutters, cut out as many shapes as possible. Place on greased baking sheets about 1 inch apart and bake for 10–15 minutes or until lightly golden. Cool on a wire rack.

Illustrated on page 98

Greek Pastry Twists

KATIMERIA

This is a simple recipe from Crete. Traditionally these twists are fried in oil and then drenched in a syrup of honey and sugar. However, I prefer to sprinkle them with sugar and bake in the oven. They are light and crispy.

MAKES 70–80

½ oz compressed yeast, or 1 package active dry yeast
1 tsp + ¾ cup sugar
¼ cup lukewarm water
1½ sticks (6 oz) butter, melted
1 egg
½ cup orange juice
1 tbsp grated orange zest
3¼ cups all-purpose flour

Place the yeast, 1 tsp sugar and warm water in a small bowl. If compressed yeast, cream together; if dry stir to dissolve. Set aside in a warm place for 15–20 minutes or until the mixture begins to froth.

Pour the butter into a large bowl and stir in the egg, orange juice, orange zest and yeast mixture. Gradually sift in the flour and mix until you have a soft dough. Transfer to a lightly floured work surface and knead for about 10 minutes or until smooth. (Alternatively, knead the dough using the dough hook in a heavy duty (countertop) electric mixer.) Divide the dough into two equal portions and wrap each in foil. Refrigerate for several hours.

Preheat the oven to 350°F.

Remove the dough from the refrigerator, unwrap and leave for 10 minutes.

Divide the remaining sugar in half and sprinkle a little of it over the work surface. Take one portion of dough and roll it out into a rectangle about ⅛ inch thick. Sprinkle some of the sugar over its surface, fold in half and roll out to a rectangle again. Repeat this process twice more, sprinkling the work surface and surface of the dough with a little sugar each time.

Cut the final rectangle into strips about ¾ × 3 inches. Sprinkle any remaining sugar over them. Using the thumb and forefinger of each hand pick up each strip and twist into a spiral. Place on greased baking sheets, about ½ inch apart.

Repeat with the remaining ball of dough and portion of sugar.

Bake for about 15 minutes or until lightly golden. Remove and cool on wire racks before storing in an airtight tin.

Illustrated on page 99

98

Cookies with Poppy Seeds

Greek Pastry Twists

Breads

Cinnamon Bread

SHUSHI NAZUG

"Hunger sees nothing but bread." – Turkish saying

A *delicious aromatic sweet bread, this can be eaten for breakfast or as a snack with tea or coffee. This is one of many versions, some of which are made with fillings such as toasted flour, spices, nuts or dates.*

MAKES 4 SMALL LOAVES

½ oz compressed yeast, or 1 package active dry yeast
¼ cup lukewarm milk
2 eggs, lightly beaten
1½ sticks (6 oz) butter, melted and cooled
6 tbsp sugar
½ tsp salt
2 tsp ground cinnamon
1 tsp vanilla extract
3¼ cups all-purpose flour
1 egg, beaten, to glaze

Put the yeast and milk in a large bowl. If compressed yeast, cream together; if dry, stir to dissolve.

Mix in the eggs, butter, sugar, salt, cinnamon and vanilla. Gradually sift in the flour and mix until you have a soft dough. Transfer to a lightly floured work surface and knead for 10–15 minutes or until the dough is smooth and elastic. (Alternatively, knead the dough using the dough hook in a heavy duty (countertop) electric mixer.)

Wash and dry the mixing bowl and grease it with a little oil. Add the dough and roll it around the bowl until coated with the oil. This will prevent the surface from cracking. Cover the bowl with a cloth and leave to rise in a warm place overnight or for at least 6–8 hours until doubled in bulk.

Punch down the dough and knead for a few minutes. Divide it into four portions and roll each one into a ball. Press out each ball into a round about ½ inch thick. Place on greased baking sheets about 2 inches apart and leave in a warm place to rise for another 30 minutes.

Preheat the oven to 375°F.

Glaze the top of each loaf with the beaten egg and bake for 10–15 minutes or until cooked through.

Berber Semolina Bread

— REKHISS —

This North African bread, a favorite of the Berber people, is found throughout Morocco, Algeria and Tunisia where it is also known as hasha or matlou. Its basic ingredient is semolina flour which makes a coarse and delicious bread.

MAKES 3 LOAVES

½ oz compressed yeast, or 1 package active dry yeast
1 tsp sugar
3–4 tbsp lukewarm water
6½ cups semolina flour
1 tsp salt
¾ cup semolina flour, to coat

Place the yeast, sugar and water in a small bowl. If compressed yeast, cream together; if dry, stir to dissolve. Set aside in a warm place for 15–20 minutes or until the mixture begins to froth.

Sift the semolina flour and salt into a large bowl and make a well in the center. Add the yeast mixture and enough extra water to make a stiff dough. Transfer to a floured work surface and knead for at least 10 minutes or until the dough is soft and elastic. (Alternatively, knead the dough using the dough hook in a heavy duty (countertop) electric mixer.)

Divide the dough into three and roll each portion into a smooth ball. Roll each ball in the extra semolina until well coated. Sprinkle any semolina that remains over the work surface, place the balls of dough on it and cover with a dish towel. Leave to rise for 1–2 hours or until doubled in bulk.

Preheat the oven to 350°F.

Heat three greased baking sheets over a low heat, then place a ball of dough on each. Gently flatten each one to a ½–¾ inch thickness. Use the tines of a fork to prick the surface in several places.

Bake for 30–40 minutes or until golden. Remove from the oven, transfer to wire racks and leave until cold before serving.

Flaky Armenian Bread

———— BLOR KETEH ————

*T*his delicious flaky bread is best eaten warm, either on its own or with jam, honey or cheese. It is traditionally served on the breakfast table the morning after a wedding.

MAKES 6 SMALL LOAVES

½ oz compressed yeast, or	*To finish*
1 package active dry yeast	6 tbsp unsalted butter, melted
4 tsp sugar	1 small egg, beaten
½ cup lukewarm water	sesame seeds or black cumin seeds
3¼ cups all-purpose flour	
¾ cup lukewarm evaporated milk	
1 egg, beaten	
1 tsp salt	
3 tbsp unsalted butter, melted	

Place the yeast, 1 tsp sugar and warm water in a small bowl. If compressed yeast, cream together; if dry, stir to dissolve. Set aside in a warm place for 15–20 minutes or until the mixture begins to froth.

Sift the flour into a large bowl. Place all the remaining ingredients, including the rest of the sugar, in another bowl and stir well. Make a well in the center of the flour and pour in the yeast mixture and the milk mixture. Work in the flour and when a dough is formed, transfer to a work surface. Knead for about 10 minutes or until soft and shiny.

Grease a large bowl with a little butter and place the dough in it. Cover with a clean dish towel and set aside in a warm place to rise for 1½–2 hours or until the dough has doubled in bulk.

Punch down the dough, return to a floured work surface and knead for a few more minutes. Divide the dough into six equal portions, roll into balls and cover with a cloth.

Flour the work surface. Take one ball of dough and roll it out into a thin round about 12–14 inches in diameter. Brush the surface with some of the melted butter. Roll up the round to form a long rope. Hold each end gently and swing the pastry up and down, letting the dough hit the work surface. This will double the length of the rope. Coil the rope around and press the outside end on top of the outer coil. Use your hand or a rolling pin to flatten into a 6 inch round. Place on a greased baking sheet. Repeat with the remaining balls of dough.

Leave to rise in a warm place for a further 30–45 minutes or until the dough has risen.

Preheat the oven to 375°F.

Brush the tops of the breads with beaten egg and sprinkle with the sesame seeds or cumin seeds. Bake for 12–15 minutes or until golden and cooked. Cool on a wire rack.

 Cypriot Olive Buns

ELIOPITTA

"An unfortunate year is that in which there is no wheat or olives." – Moroccan saying

A specialty of the island of Cyprus, these small round olive and cheese buns are traditionally served during Easter Saturday and Sunday. They are also served as part of a funeral feast. Delicious when warm.

MAKES 8

½ oz compressed yeast, or 1 package active dry yeast
1 tsp sugar
5–6 tbsp + 1¼ cups lukewarm water
3¼ cups all-purpose flour
1 tsp salt
3–4 tbsp olive oil
1 cup roughly chopped black olives
½ lb haloumi or Cheddar cheese, coarsely chopped

Place the yeast, sugar and 5–6 tbsp water in a small bowl. If compressed yeast, cream together; if dry, stir to dissolve. Leave in a warm place for 15–20 minutes or until it begins to froth.

Sift the flour and salt into a large bowl and make a well in the center. Add the yeast mixture and remaining warm water and knead to form a firm dough. Transfer to a floured work surface and knead for 10–15 minutes or until smooth and elastic. (Alternatively, knead the dough using the dough hook in a heavy duty (countertop) electric mixer.)

Wash and dry the mixing bowl and grease it with a little of the olive oil. Add the dough and roll it around the bowl until well greased. Cover the bowl with a clean dish towel and leave to rise in a warm place for about 2 hours or until doubled in bulk.

Punch down the dough and return to the work surface. Add the olives and cheese and knead in thoroughly. Grease your hands with olive oil and then divide the dough into eight portions. Roll each between your palms into a ball. Keeping your hands greased, flatten each ball until 3–4 inches in diameter. Dust the tops with a little flour, cover with a cloth and leave to rise in a warm place for a further 45 minutes.

Preheat the oven to 450°F.

Place the buns on oiled baking sheets and bake for 12–15 minutes or until golden. Serve while warm.

Illustrated on page 106

Greek Holiday Bread

─── TSOUREKI ───

This bread is eaten at Easter and Christmas time. Ground mastic is added to the dough to give it its distinctive "Greek" character.

MAKES 2 LOAVES

½ oz compressed yeast, or	*To finish*
1 package active dry yeast	1 egg, beaten
1 tsp + ¼ cup sugar	sesame seeds
2 tbsp lukewarm water	
3¼ cups all-purpose flour	
pinch of salt	
½ tsp ground mastic (page 8)	
1 stick butter, melted	
⅔ cup lukewarm milk	
2 eggs, beaten	

Place the yeast, 1 tsp sugar and the warm water in a small bowl. If compressed yeast, cream together; if dry, stir to dissolve. Set aside in a warm place for 15–20 minutes or until the mixture begins to froth.

Sift the flour and salt into a large bowl and stir in the remaining sugar and the mastic. Make a well in the center and add the yeast mixture, butter, milk and eggs. Blend the flour into the liquids with a metal spoon until a dough is formed. Gather it up into a ball and transfer to a lightly floured work surface. Knead for about 10 minutes or until the dough is smooth and elastic. (Alternatively, knead the dough using the dough hook in a heavy duty (countertop) electric mixer.)

Put in a clean bowl, cover with a dish towel and set aside in a warm place to rise for about 2 hours or until the dough has doubled in bulk.

Punch down the dough, transfer to the work surface and knead for 1–2 minutes. Divide the dough into six equal portions. Take three and roll each into a sausage about 8 inches long. Braid together loosely and lift carefully onto a greased baking sheet. Repeat with the remaining three portions of dough. Cover both loaves with clean dish towels and leave in a warm place to rise for a further 30 minutes.

Preheat the oven to 350°F.

Brush the loaves with the beaten egg and sprinkle with sesame seeds. Brush again with the egg, then bake for about 30 minutes or until golden and cooked. Remove and cool on wire racks.

Illustrated on page 107

Cypriot Olive Buns

Greek Holiday Bread

Turkish Festive Bread topped with Sesame and Fennel Seeds

— PIDE —

This Turkish bread is usually prepared during the festive season of Bayram (Muslim Ramadan). It is related to the famed bread of the "Franks and Armenians" which is mentioned in the great eleventh-century cookbook of Al-Baghdadi.

MAKES 1 LARGE LOAF

1 oz compressed yeast, or	*Topping*
2 packages active dry yeast	1 egg, beaten
1 tsp + 3 tbsp sugar	3½ tbsp sesame seeds
1 cup lukewarm water	1½ tsp fennel seeds
4 tbsp butter or margarine	
¾ cup milk	
4¾ cups all-purpose flour	
1 tbsp salt	

Place the yeast, 1 tsp sugar and ¼ cup of the warm water in a small bowl. If compressed yeast, cream together; if dry, stir to dissolve. Set aside in a warm place for 15–20 minutes or until the mixture begins to froth.

Place the butter, milk and remaining water in a small saucepan and heat slowly until the butter has melted. Remove from the heat.

Sift the flour and salt into a large bowl and stir in the remaining sugar. Make a well in the center and add the yeast and butter mixtures. Gradually work in the flour until a soft dough is formed. Transfer to a floured work surface and knead for about 10 minutes or until smooth and elastic. (Alternatively, knead the dough using the dough hook in a heavy duty (countertop) electric mixer.)

Grease a large circular dish about 12 inches in diameter. Place the dough in the center of the dish and press it down until it forms a round loaf about 10 inches in diameter. Cover with a dish towel and leave to rise in a warm place for 1½–2 hours.

Preheat the oven to 375°F.

Brush the surface of the bread with the beaten egg and sprinkle the sesame and fennel seeds evenly over it. Using the point of a sharp knife make a pattern over the top. Bake for about 40 minutes or until golden brown and cooked through. Transfer to a wire rack and leave to cool.

Jewish Festive Bread

—————— SWEET CHALLAH ——————

*T*his *is a version of the famed braided bread of the Jews which is available in many bakeries. Sweet Challah is traditionally prepared for special holidays. The raisins give it that extra sweetness while the egg yolk provides the extra sheen to the crust. Serve with honey or jam – delicious!*

MAKES 2 LOAVES

½ oz compressed yeast, or 1 package active dry yeast
1 tsp + 3 tbsp sugar
1 cup lukewarm water
3¼ cups all-purpose flour
2 tsp salt
2 eggs
3 tbsp vegetable oil
⅓ cup raisins
1 egg yolk, beaten with 1 tbsp water, to glaze

Place the yeast and 1 tsp sugar in a small bowl and add a few tbsp of the warm water. If compressed yeast, cream together; if dry, stir to dissolve. Set aside in a warm place for 15–20 minutes or until the mixture begins to froth.

Sift the flour and salt into a large bowl and make a well in the center. Add the yeast mixture, remaining sugar, eggs and the rest of the water. Gradually draw the flour into the liquid and mix until a dough is formed. Add the oil and raisins and work in thoroughly. Transfer the dough to a floured work surface and knead for about 10 minutes until the dough is smooth and elastic. (Alternatively, knead the dough using the dough hook in a heavy duty (countertop) electric mixer.) Roll into a ball.

Lightly oil a large bowl, add the ball of dough and roll it around until evenly coated with the oil. Cover with a dish towel and set aside in a warm place to rise for about 2 hours or until doubled in bulk.

Return the dough to the work surface, punch down and knead for 2–3 minutes. Return the dough to the bowl, cover and leave in a warm place to rise for a further 45 minutes.

Transfer the dough to the work surface, knock back and then divide into two portions. Roll out each one into a sausage about 2 feet long. Curl each one around into a snail shape and place on a greased baking sheet. Cover with a damp dish towel and leave in the warm place to rise for a further 30 minutes.

Preheat the oven to 350°F.

Brush the loaves with the egg yolk glaze. Bake for about 45 minutes or until cooked and golden. Remove and cool on wire racks.

North African Festive Bread

KHOBZ EL-EID

In Morocco this bread is baked on the first day of the academic year, when a loaf is given to each child on the morning of the first day of school. It often comes with a hard-cooked egg.

MAKES 6 LOAVES

½ oz compressed yeast, or 1 package active dry yeast
1 tsp sugar
3–4 tbsp lukewarm water
3¼ cups semolina flour
3¼ cups all-purpose flour
1 tsp salt
1 stick butter, melted
1 egg
1 tbsp green aniseed, crushed or powdered
1¼ cups water
1 egg yolk, beaten, to glaze
6 hard-cooked eggs, shelled
1 tbsp each poppy seeds and sesame seeds

Place the yeast, sugar and warm water in a small bowl. If compressed yeast, cream together; if dry, stir to dissolve. Set aside in a warm place for 15–20 minutes or until the mixture begins to froth.

Sift the semolina flour, flour and salt into a large bowl. Make a well in the center and add the yeast mixture, butter, egg, aniseed and half the water. Mix well, then gradually knead in enough of the remaining water to form a soft dough. Transfer to a work surface and knead for about 10 minutes or until smooth and elastic. (Alternatively, knead the dough using the dough hook in a heavy duty (countertop) electric mixer.)

Set aside an apple-sized lump of dough to be used later as decoration. Divide the rest of the dough into six equal parts and roll each into a smooth ball. Lightly flour the work surface and roll out each ball into a round about 4–5 inches in diameter. Cover with clean dish towels and leave to rise for about 1 hour.

Preheat the oven to 350°F.

Take one bread round and decorate it with a pattern of your choice using the tines of a fork. Brush the surface with egg yolk. Place a hard-cooked egg in the center. Roll out the apple-sized lump of pastry thinly and cut into ½ inch wide strips. Place two strips at right angles across the egg and press the ends into the edge of the loaf. Brush the strips with egg and sprinkle with the poppy and sesame seeds. Repeat with the remaining loaves.

Place on greased baking sheets and bake for 25–30 minutes or until golden. Remove to wire racks and leave to cool.

oroccan Bread

— KSRA —

*Ksra, the daily bread of Morocco, is made with both all-purpose flour and semolina flour
and is spiced with aniseed which gives it a slightly aromatic flavor.
It is marvelous eaten on its own or with cheese, honey or any fruit preserve.*

MAKES 3 LOAVES

½ oz compressed yeast, or 1 package active dry yeast
1 tsp sugar
1½ cups lukewarm water
3¼ cups semolina flour
3¼ cups all-purpose flour
1 tsp salt
1½ sticks (6 oz) butter, melted
zest of 1 orange, finely chopped
1 tbsp green aniseed
2 tbsp sesame seeds
2 eggs, beaten
1 egg yolk, beaten, to glaze

Place the yeast, sugar and ¼ cup warm water in a small bowl. If compressed yeast, cream together; if dry, stir to dissolve. Set aside in a warm place for 15–20 minutes or until the mixture begins to froth.

Sift the semolina flour, flour and salt into a large bowl. Make a well in the center and add the yeast mixture, butter, orange zest, aniseed, sesame seeds and half the remaining water. Gradually work the dry ingredients into the liquid. Knead in the eggs and remaining water to make a soft dough. Add a little more water if necessary. Transfer to a floured work surface and knead for about 10 minutes or until smooth and elastic. (Alternatively, knead the dough using the dough hook in a heavy duty (countertop) electric mixer.)

Divide the dough into three and roll each into a ball. Cover with a dish towel and leave to rise in a warm place for 1–2 hours or until the dough has doubled in bulk.

Preheat the oven to 350°F.

Place each ball of dough on a greased baking sheet and gently flatten until about 1 inch thick. Brush the surfaces with the egg yolk glaze. Bake for 30–40 minutes or until golden. Remove and cool on wire racks.

Lebanese Thyme Bread

──── MANNAEESH ────

Sold by street vendors, Mannaeesh Zahtar comes in a variety of differing shapes. Excellent for breakfast or as a snack at any time.

MAKES 10

½ oz compressed yeast, or 1 package active dry yeast
1 tsp sugar
1¼ cups lukewarm water
3¼ cups all-purpose flour
½ tsp salt
6 tbsp olive oil
2 heaped tsp dried thyme
1 heaped tsp dried marjoram
3 tbsp sesame seeds

Place the yeast and sugar in a small bowl and stir in a few tbsp of the warm water. If compressed yeast, cream together; if dry, stir to dissolve. Leave in a warm place for 15–20 minutes or until the mixture begins to froth.

Sift the flour and salt into a large bowl and make a well in the center. Add the yeast mixture and remaining warm water and knead until you have a firm dough. Transfer to a floured work surface and continue to knead for 10–15 minutes or until smooth and elastic. (Alternatively, knead the dough using the dough hook in a heavy duty (countertop) electric mixer.) During this time knead 1 tbsp olive oil into the dough – this will make it softer.

Wash and dry the mixing bowl and grease with a little oil. Add the dough and roll around the bowl until well oiled. Cover with a clean cloth and leave in a warm place to rise for about 2 hours or until doubled in bulk.

Punch down the dough and knead for a few minutes. Divide it into 10 portions and roll each between your palms until smooth and round. Flour the work surface. Flatten each round with a rolling pin until it is circular, even and about ¼ inch thick. Cover and leave in a warm place to rise for a further 20 minutes.

Preheat the oven to 450°F. Put two large, oiled baking sheets in the oven to heat.

Brush the tops of the rounds with a little of the olive oil. Mix the remaining oil with the thyme, marjoram and sesame seeds in a small bowl and spread this mixture over the surface of each round.

Slide the bread onto the hot baking sheets and bake for 8–10 minutes. Remove from the oven and put on wire racks to cool.

Festive Cakes

─ KAAHK EL-RAMAZAN ─

MAKES ABOUT 20

½ oz compressed yeast, or	*Topping*
1 package active dry yeast	1 egg, beaten, to glaze
1 cup lukewarm milk	choice of 2 of the following:
3 tbsp sugar	1 tbsp poppy seeds, 1 tbsp sesame
3¼ cups all-purpose flour	seeds, 1 tbsp chopped almonds,
1 tsp salt	1 tbsp chopped pine nuts
½ tsp ground cinnamon, or 1 tsp	
vanilla extract or rosewater	
10 tbsp unsalted butter, chilled	
2 eggs, beaten	

Place the yeast in a small bowl with a few tbsp of the warm milk and 1 tbsp of the sugar. If compressed yeast, cream together; if dry, stir to dissolve. Leave in a warm place for 15–20 minutes or until frothy.

Sift the flour, salt and cinnamon (if using) into a large bowl and stir in the remaining sugar. Add 2 tbsp of the butter, cut into small pieces, and rub in until the mixture resembles fine bread crumbs. Make a well in the center and add the yeast mixture, remaining milk, beaten eggs and the vanilla or rosewater (if using). Gradually draw the flour into the liquid and mix until you have a soft, smooth dough. Cover the bowl with a damp cloth and refrigerate for 1 hour.

Place the remaining butter between two sheets of wax paper and, using a rolling pin, roll out the butter into a rectangle 6 × 4 inches. Refrigerate the flattened butter.

Remove the dough from the refrigerator and knead for a further 5 minutes. Transfer to a lightly floured work surface and roll out into an oblong about 12 × 8 inches.

Remove the butter from the refrigerator, unwrap and place in the center of the dough. Carefully fold over the four sides of the dough to enclose the butter completely. Roll out into a strip 12–15 inches long. Fold the bottom third up to the center and the top third down to the center. Refrigerate, wrapped, for 15 minutes. Repeat the rolling out, folding and refrigerating twice more, then refrigerate for 1 hour.

Roll out the dough to a rectangle about 24 × 16 inches and about ¼ inch thick. Cut the dough down the middle and then cut each half into three 8 inch squares. Cut each square in half diagonally to form triangles. Roll each triangle up quite tightly from the broadest edge to the tip. Pull into a crescent shape and join the two ends together. Place on ungreased baking sheets, with the central tips underneath to prevent unrolling. Cover with a damp cloth and leave to rise for 20–30 minutes.

Preheat the oven to 425°F.

Separate the joined ends but leave in crescent shapes. Brush with the egg glaze. Sprinkle half with one topping, half with the other. Bake for about 10 minutes or until golden brown. Cool on wire racks.

Small Round Israeli Breads

———— BAGEL-LIKE PRETZELS ————

This is an Israeli version of a famed Ashkenazim Jewish bread called bagels. It includes both caraway and sesame seeds in place of poppy seeds. Serve warm.

MAKES 30–36

½ oz compressed yeast, or	*To finish*
1 package active dry yeast	1 egg, beaten with 1 tbsp water,
1 tsp sugar	to glaze
¼ cup lukewarm water	sesame seeds
3¼ cups all-purpose flour	
1 tsp salt	
1 tsp caraway seeds	
1½ sticks (6 oz) margarine, melted	
½ cup vegetable oil	

Place the yeast and sugar in a small bowl with the water. If compressed yeast, cream together; if dry, stir to dissolve. Leave in a warm place for 15–20 minutes or until the mixture begins to froth.

Sift the flour and salt into a large bowl and stir in the caraway seeds. Make a well in the center and add the yeast mixture, melted margarine and oil. Gradually mix the flour into the liquid until a dough is formed. Transfer to a floured work surface and knead for about 10 minutes or until smooth and elastic. (Alternatively, knead the dough using the dough hook in a heavy duty (countertop) electric mixer.)

Place the dough in a clean bowl, cover with a dish towel and leave in a warm place to rise for about 2 hours or until doubled in bulk.

Preheat the oven to 375°F.

Punch down the dough and knead for 2–3 minutes. Divide the dough into 30–36 portions and roll each into a ball. Roll each ball into a sausage about 5 inches long. Bring the ends together and press one on top of the other to secure. Place on ungreased baking sheets. Brush with the egg yolk glaze and sprinkle generously with sesame seeds. Bake for about 20 minutes or until cooked and lightly browned.

Illustrated on page 118

Kurdish Pumpkin Bread

— NOUNE KADU FERANGHI —

This is an unusual bread from the mountains of Kurdistan. It is moist and spicy with a texture more akin to cake. It is excellent with thick Middle Eastern cream (page 125), butter, honey or jam. The Kurds and Persians have other tasty breads including onion bread and spinach bread.

MAKES 1 LOAF

½ lb peeled and seeded pumpkin flesh (about 2 cups grated)
2 eggs, beaten until frothy
½ cup vegetable oil
6 tbsp cold water
2½ cups all-purpose flour
2 tsp baking powder
½ tsp salt
¾ tsp ground cinnamon
1 tsp grated nutmeg
½ cup sugar

Preheat the oven to 350°F. Grease and flour a 9 × 5 × 3 inch loaf pan.

Grate the pumpkin flesh into a large bowl. Add the beaten eggs, oil and water and mix well. Sift the flour, baking powder, salt, cinnamon and nutmeg into another bowl. Gradually stir this into the pumpkin mixture, together with the sugar and mix until thoroughly blended.

Pour into the loaf pan and smooth over the surface with the back of a spoon. Bake for about 1 hour or until well risen and cooked through.

Unmold onto a wire rack and leave to cool.

Illustrated on page 119

Small Round Israeli Breads

Kurdish Pumpkin Bread

Basic Recipes

Paper-Thin Pastry Sheets

BAKLAVA FILO

Commercial filo pastry is now readily available in most parts of the country. It comes in 1 lb packages and can be bought from large supermarkets, specialty food stores, and Middle Eastern food stores. Much filo pastry is sold frozen and should be thawed slowly at room temperature before unrolling carefully. It becomes brittle quickly when exposed to the air so keep it covered with a sheet of wax paper and a damp dish towel.

Different commercial companies make their sheets of filo in different sizes. When preparing a baklava in a pan, you may find that instead of following the instructions in the recipe, you will have to use a whole sheet for each layer. In this case, trim them to fit the pan and slip the trimmings in between the layers as you proceed.

This pastry is thin and excellent for use in all the baklava recipes in this book. However, commercial filo is still not as thin as that prepared by the pâtissiers of the Middle East. Therefore, I have included below a recipe which explains how to prepare your own filo pastry.

MAKES 18 SHEETS

4¾ cups all-purpose flour
1 tsp salt
2 cups warm water
3 tbsp olive oil
cornstarch, to dust

Sift the flour and salt into a large bowl and make a well in the center. Little by little add the warm water, kneading until you have a soft dough. Gather up into a ball, transfer to a lightly floured work surface and knead for at least 5 minutes.

Work in the oil, 1 tbsp at a time, and continue kneading for at least 20 minutes, by which time the dough should be smooth and satiny.

Wash and dry the mixing bowl. Place the ball of dough in it and cover with a dish towel. Set aside to rest for about 4 hours.

Divide the dough into 18 equal portions and roll each between your palms to form a ball. Lightly dust the work surface with cornstarch. Taking one ball at a time, roll it out into a round about 6–7 inches in diameter. Place the first round on wax paper and stack the others on top of it. Cover with a damp cloth and leave to rest for about 45 minutes.

To shape a sheet, take one round of dough and stretch it over the backs of your hands: pull your hands carefully apart stretching the dough out until it is uniformly paper thin. You must work carefully but quickly because the dough dries quickly. When you have managed to stretch a sheet to about 12 × 18–20 inches, dust the work surface with cornstarch again and lay the sheet out flat. Trim off the thick edges to make a rectangle about 11 × 16 inches. Set aside and cover immediately with wax paper and a damp cloth. Prepare the remaining sheets in the same way.

$\mathcal{S}$hredded Pastry

KUNAFEH FILO

*T*his *pastry looks rather like a fine shredded wheat. It is not as readily available as baklava filo,
but can be found in many Middle Eastern food stores. If it is bought frozen,
let it thaw slowly at room temperature before using.
For convenience sake, use commercial pastry. But for the truly adventurous, here is a recipe for
home-made kunafeh pastry. You need two pieces of basic equipment – a large metal griddle and a
kunaffahiah, a deep dish with numerous small holes through which the batter
is dropped onto the hot griddle.*

MAKES ABOUT 1 lb

4¾ **cups all-purpose flour**
1¼ **cups warm water**
1¼ **cups milk**

Sift the flour into a large bowl and make a well in the center. Gradually add the water and work into the flour. Then, little by little, add the milk and continue to knead until you have a smooth dough. Thin the mixture by gradually adding more water (about 2 cups), stirring all the time, until the mixture forms a smooth batter. It should have the consistency of thin cream.

Place a large metal griddle over a low heat.

With a large soup ladle, pour some of the batter into the *kunaffahiah* held over the griddle. The batter will drop onto the hot griddle in a thin rope-like form and solidify in a few seconds. Lift the cooked pastry into a large bowl and continue until all the batter has been used.

North African Paper-Thin Pastry Sheets

OUARKA or DIOUL

Wherever ouarka or dioul is traditionally used in a recipe, I suggest that, for convenience sake, you substitute baklava filo. Ouarka is a very thin dough that is time-consuming to make. However, if you wish to try it then here is a standard recipe.

MAKES 12 SHEETS

1¼ cups semolina flour
1¼ cups all-purpose flour, sifted
¼ tsp salt
2½ cups water
7–8 tbsp olive oil

Put the semolina flour and flour in a large bowl, add the salt and half the water and knead for several minutes. Now, little by little add the remaining water, stirring continuously, until it has all been absorbed. Continue kneading for at least 10 minutes, lifting the batter and beating it against the sides of the bowl. The batter should be just liquid enough to find its own level. Cover the batter with $\frac{1}{16}$ inch water and leave to rest for about 1 hour.

Fill a large deep saucepan that is about 10 inches in diameter three-quarters full with water. Invert a large, heavy-based skillet over it and bring the water to a boil over a moderate heat.

Brush the base of the inverted hot pan with a little of the oil, then wipe with a clean cloth or paper towel so that there is only a light film of oil left on the surface. Lightly wet your hands with cold water and scoop up a handful of the batter. Tap the hot pan with the batter by lowering and raising your hand regularly – the batter will be deftly caught as it touches the hot surface and will leave a fine layer each time. Take care not to burn your fingertips. When the pan is covered with batter, remove the pastry sheet by lifting it with a palette knife and place it on a clean cloth, shiny side up (this will prevent the sheets from sticking to each other). Lightly re-oil the pan between preparing each sheet of pastry, and stack the cooked sheets on top of each other. Wrap in a clean cloth to prevent them drying.

The pastry sheets will keep for 2–3 days if the edges are brushed with a little oil and they are wrapped in a cloth and then foil.

Clarified Butter

— SUSME YEG or SMEN —

In Turkey, clarified butter is called sūsme yeğ; it is smen in Arabic. The Indian butter called ghee is a type of clarified butter and is commercially available, but it is easy to prepare your own. Clarified butter does not burn at high temperatures and it can be kept, refrigerated, for up to a year. It is used extensively in Middle Eastern desserts and pastries.

MAKES ABOUT 1½ lb

2 lb unsalted butter

Melt the butter in a saucepan over a low heat. Use a metal spoon to skim off the foam as it rises to the surface. Remove the pan from the heat and set aside to cool for 5 minutes. Skim off any more foam that appears.

Spoon the clear butter into a bowl and discard the milky residue at the bottom of the pan. Refrigerate the butter until hard.

Syrups

"Sugar did not fall into water in order to melt." – Caucasian saying

In the old days, and still today in North Africa, honey was used as the sweetener for all pastries. Today, sugar-based syrups are most commonly used with pastries. The sugar and water are boiled with a little lemon juice to prevent crystallization. Then the syrup is often flavored with rosewater (Middle East) or orange blossom water (North Africa).

Syrup I

MAKES ABOUT 2 cups

1¾ cups sugar
1 tbsp lemon juice
1½ cups water
2 tbsp rosewater

Place the sugar, lemon juice and water in a saucepan and bring to a boil, stirring to dissolve the sugar. Lower the heat and simmer for about 10 minutes or until the syrup leaves a slightly sticky film on a metal spoon.

Remove from the heat, stir in the rosewater and set aside until ready to use.

Syrup II

MAKES ABOUT 2 cups

1¾ cups sugar
1 tbsp lemon juice
1½ cups water
½ tsp ground allspice
1 tbsp rosewater
1 tbsp orange blossom water

Prepare the syrup as described above, then remove from the heat and stir in the allspice, rosewater and orange blossom water.

Middle Eastern Cream

KAYMAK

This thick cream can be cut with a knife. It is usually prepared with buffalo's milk, but can also be made with cow's milk or even goat's. It is delicious on its own topped with sugar, jam or honey, or serve it as a topping for pastries.

MAKES ABOUT ¾ cup

3¾ cups creamy milk
1¼ cups heavy cream

Pour the milk and cream into a large shallow pan, stir well and bring slowly to a boil. Lower the heat and simmer very gently for about 2 hours. Remove from the heat and leave for 6–8 hours.

Now refrigerate for several hours, after which time a thick layer of cream will have formed. Using a sharp knife, free the edges of this layer and cut it into strips. Use a spatula to remove the strips to a large plate and then cut into squares or curl into rolls.

Index

Note Page numbers in italics refer
to illustrations

index

The Scale Of Things

The Scale of

LANDFORMS

Joanna Brundle

Crabtree Publishing Company

www.crabtreebooks.com

CRABTREE
PUBLISHING COMPANY
WWW.CRABTREEBOOKS.COM

Author: Joanna Brundle

Editorial director: Kathy Middleton

Editors: Emilie Dufresne, Janine Deschenes

Design: Jasmine Pointer

Proofreader: Crystal Sikkens

Prepress technician: Tammy McGarr

Print coordinator: Katherine Berti

All facts, statistics, web addresses and URLs in this book were verified as valid and accurate at time of writing.
No responsibility for any changes to external websites or references can be accepted by either the author or publisher.

Image Credits

All images courtesy of Shutterstock.com. With thanks to Getty Images, Thinkstock Photo and iStockphoto.

Front Cover – Bluehousestudio, robuart, Moloko88, Ilyafs, runLenarun. 2–3 Amanita Silvicora. 4–5 – asantosg. 6–7 – Tomacco. 8–9 – ginger1, Anastasia Boiko. 10–11 – labzazuza. 12–13 – Fancy Tapis, JBOY, VectorShow, Panda Vector. 14–15 – LineTale, FMStox. 16–17 – SaveJungle, Sentavio. 18–19 – MicroOne, Dark ink. 20–21 – Chalintra.B, Katrevich Valeriy. 22–23 – Ksenica Artbox.

Library and Archives Canada Cataloguing in Publication

Title: The scale of landforms / Joanna Brundle.
Other titles: Scale of natural landmarks
Names: Brundle, Joanna, author.
Description: Series statement: The scale of things |
    Previously published under title: The scale of natural landmarks. King's Lynn,
    Norfolk : BookLife Publishing, 2019. | Includes index.
Identifiers: Canadiana (print) 20190191899 | Canadiana (ebook) 20190191902 |
    ISBN 9780778776574 (hardcover) |
    ISBN 9780778776758 (softcover) |
    ISBN 9781427125293 (HTML)
Subjects: LCSH: Landforms—Juvenile literature. | LCSH: Natural monuments—
    Juvenile literature. | LCSH: Measurement—Juvenile literature. |
    LCSH: Size perception—Juvenile literature. | LCSH: Size judgment—
    Juvenile literature.
Classification: LCC GB404 .B78 2020 | DDC j551.41—dc23

Library of Congress Cataloging-in-Publication Data

CIP available at the Library of Congress

LCCN: 2019043841

Crabtree Publishing Company
www.crabtreebooks.com   1–800–387–7650
Published by Crabtree Publishing Company in 2020

©2019 BookLife Publishing Ltd.

Printed in the U.S.A./012020/CG20191115

Published in Canada
Crabtree Publishing
616 Welland Ave.
St. Catharines, Ontario
L2M 5V6

Published in the United States
Crabtree Publishing
PMB 59051
350 Fifth Avenue, 59th Floor
New York, New York 10118

CONTENTS

Words that are in **bold** can be found in the glossary on page 24.

INTRODUCTION

Height is a measurement of how tall, or high, something is.

Length is a measurement of how long something is.

The scale of things means how one thing compares in size to another. In this book, we will travel around the world to compare famous landforms by their heights and lengths.

4

We will measure **most landforms** in feet and meters (m). The tallest trees on Earth, giant sequoias, are around 250 feet (76 m) tall. The tallest landforms will be measured in miles and kilometers (km). There are 5,280 feet in one mile and 1,000 meters in one kilometer. Use these measurements to help you imagine the heights of these landforms.

Landforms are natural shapes in the land. Some are so big that they can be seen from a long way away. Some measurements in this book are **approximate**. You can read the measurements that match the ones you learn in school.

NIAGARA FALLS

Niagara Falls is a waterfall on the Niagara River, between New York state and Ontario, Canada. At its highest point, on the Canadian side, it is 188 feet (57 m) high.

Niagara Falls is taller than 13 double decker buses piled on top of one another.

188 feet (57 m)

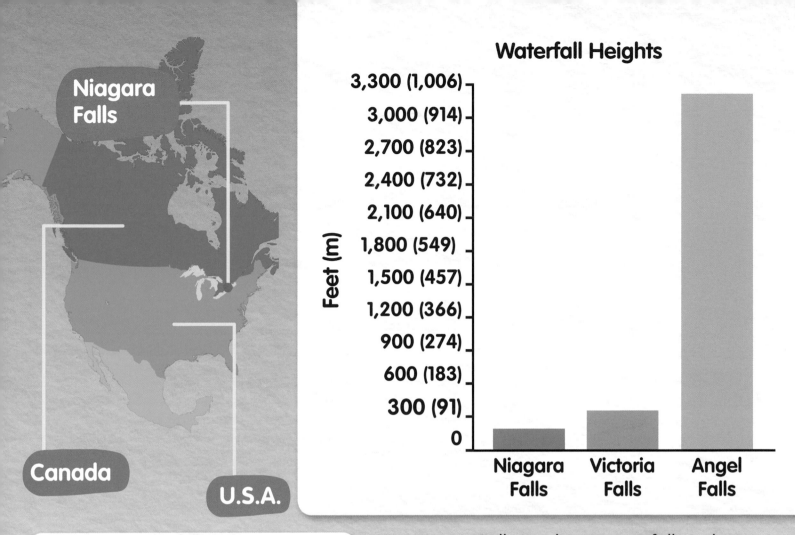

Waterfall Heights

Feet (m)	Niagara Falls	Victoria Falls	Angel Falls

(Chart y-axis labels: 3,300 (1,006); 3,000 (914); 2,700 (823); 2,400 (732); 2,100 (640); 1,800 (549); 1,500 (457); 1,200 (366); 900 (274); 600 (183); 300 (91); 0)

Niagara Falls

Canada

U.S.A.

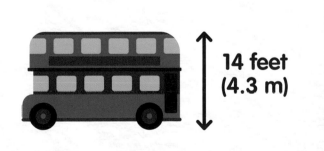

14 feet (4.3 m)

Victoria Falls is a huge waterfall on the Zambezi River in Africa. At 355 feet (108 m), it is almost twice as high as Niagara Falls. Angel Falls in Venezuela is the highest waterfall in the world. It reaches 3,212 feet (979 m)! That's more than **17 TIMES** higher than Niagara Falls.

THE WHITE CLIFFS OF DOVER AND THE CLIFFS OF MOHER

The White Cliffs of Dover are part of the **coastline** of England. The cliffs are white because they are made of **chalk**. In some spots, they are more than 350 feet (107 m) high. That's almost twice as high as Niagara Falls.

350 feet (107 m)

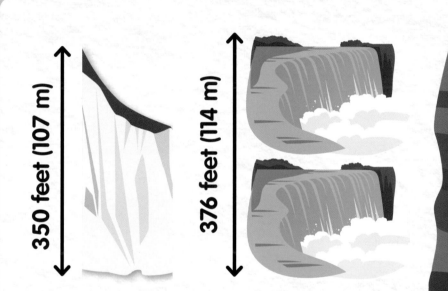

350 feet (107 m)

376 feet (114 m)

The White Cliffs of Dover

The Cliffs of Moher are in Ireland. They rise 702 feet (214 m) from the ground to their highest point. That's more than twice as high as the White Cliffs of Dover!

The Cliffs of Moher

702 feet (214 m)

The Cliffs of Moher cover around 9 miles (14.5 km) of the coastline.

HYPERION

Hyperion is taller than 27 double decker buses stacked on top of one another.

Do you know the name of the tallest tree in the world? Hyperion is a **giant redwood,** which is a type of sequoia tree. It is around 380 feet (116 m) tall!

380 feet (116 m)

Hyperion is found in a redwood-tree forest in California. **Scientists** think that the huge tree is at least 600 years old.

California

Hyperion is taller than 68 adult humans standing on top of one another.

ULURU

Uluru is a giant rock in the middle of Australia. It rises 1,142 feet (348 m) above the land around it. That is **THREE TIMES** as high as Hyperion.

Australia

Uluru

1,142 feet (348 m)

Dune 7 is a **sand dune** in the Namib **desert** in Namibia, Africa. It is around 1,256 feet (383 m) high. That makes Dune 7 as tall as Uluru, plus eight double-decker buses stacked on top.

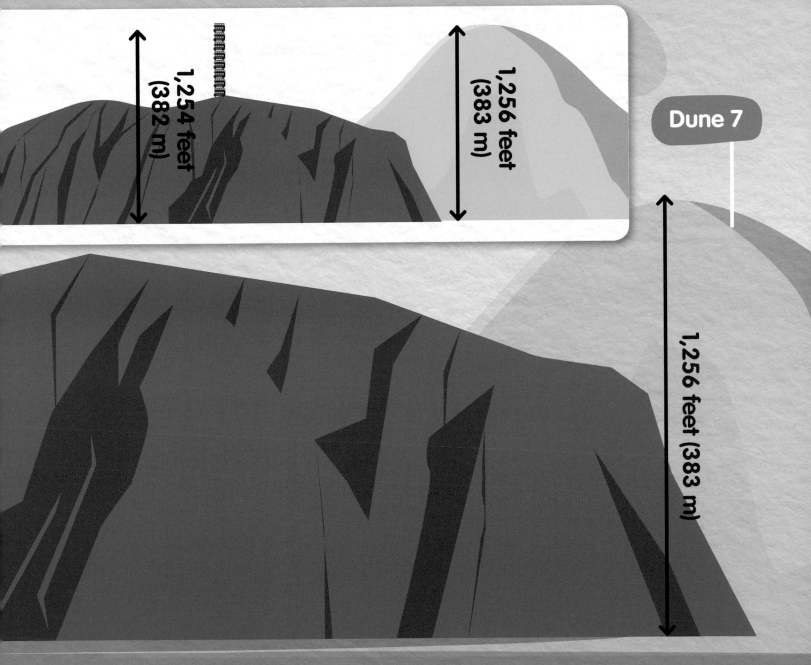

1,254 feet (382 m)

1,256 feet (383 m)

Dune 7

1,256 feet (383 m)

TABLE MOUNTAIN

Cape Town

South Africa

3,563 feet (1,086 m)

Table Mountain is a mountain that looks like a flat table top.
It towers over the city of Cape Town in South Africa.
The mountain rises to 3,563 feet (1,086 m) at its highest point.

3,426 feet
(1,044 m)

3,563 feet
(1,086 m)

Table Mountain is thought to be one
of the oldest mountains on Earth.
Its rocks are around 600 million years old.

Table Mountain
is more than
THREE TIMES higher
than Uluru.

THE GRAND CANYON

Grand Canyon

6,000 feet (1,828 m)

Colorado River

The famous Grand Canyon is in Arizona. Its **steep** sides were carved out by the Colorado River over millions of years. The Grand Canyon is 6,000 feet (1,828 m) deep at its deepest point.

The Grand Canyon is 277 miles (446 km) long. The total length of the Colorado River is 1,450 miles (2,334 km). This means the river is more than **FIVE TIMES** longer than the Grand Canyon.

Grand Canyon

Colorado River
1,450 miles
(2,334 km) long

Grand Canyon
277 miles (446 km) long

A canyon is a deep, narrow valley with steep sides. It is created when a river wears away rock.

17

MAUNA KEA

Mauna
Kea

Mauna Kea is a **volcano** in Hawaii. Mauna Kea is 13,796 feet (4,205 m) above the sea. But that's less than half of its total height! The rest of the volcano is under the sea.

The part of Mauna Kea above the sea is more than **TWICE** as tall as the Grand Canyon is deep!

13,796 feet (4,205 m)

13,796 feet (4,205 m)

12,000 feet (3,658 m)

The top of Mauna Kea is so high that the weather becomes very cold there. It is often covered in snow during winter! Some people even travel there to ski and snowboard.

Including the part under the sea, Mauna Kea is 33,500 feet (10,211 m). That's more than **FIVE TIMES** higher than the Grand Canyon is deep!

MOUNT EVEREST AND OLYMPUS MONS

29,035 feet (8,850 m)

At 29,035 feet (8,850 m) high, Mount Everest is the highest mountain in the world. It is part of a group of mountains in Asia, called the Himalayas.

Mount Everest is almost as high as five Grand Canyons stacked on top of one another.

Mount Everest

29,035 feet (8,850 m)

30,000 feet (9,144 m)

Scientists discovered a huge volcano on the planet Mars. They called it Olympus Mons. It is around 84,480 feet (25,750 m), or 16 miles (26 km), high.

Olympus Mons

16 miles (26 km)

Olympus Mons is almost THREE TIMES higher than Mount Everest.

THE GReAT BARRiER REEF AND THE YANGTZe RIVeR

Great Barrier Reef 1,615 miles (2,599 km)

The Great Barrier Reef is a massive group of coral reefs near Australia. Together, it is the largest coral reef on Earth. It can even be seen from space! The Great Barrier Reef is more than 1,615 miles (2,599 km) long.

A coral reef is a structure made from coral. Coral are sea animals. They grow hard outer skeletons that attach to each other and form the reef.

The Yangtze River in China is 3,915 miles (6,300 km) long. That means it is almost **TWO AND A HALF TIMES** longer than the Great Barrier Reef.

Yangtze River 3,915 miles (6,300 km)

The Yangtze River is the longest river in Asia. It is the third longest in the world. At 4,132 miles (6,650 km), the Nile River in Africa is the longest.

GLOSSARY

approximate Close to an exact measurement

chalk A soft, white rock that is millions of years old

coastline The area along a coast where the land meets the sea

desert A place that gets very little rain

giant redwood A very tall, evergreen tree that produces cones and has reddish wood

measure To find out the size or amount of something

measurement The number we get after measuring something

sand dune A hill of sand, formed into a variety of shapes by the wind

scientist A person who studies and has a lot of knowledge about a type of science

steep Describes something that has a very sharp downward slope

volcano A mountain that sometimes erupts, giving off very hot, melted rock and gases

INDEX